HIDDEN MEMORIES

The personal recollections of survivors and

witnesses to the Holocaust living in Ireland

Mary Rose Doorly

BLACKWATER PRESS

Editor
Rachel O'Connor

Design & Layout
Paula Byrne

ISBN
0 86121 524 9

© Mary Rose Doorly

Published in 1994 by Blackwater Press,
Broomhill Business Park,
Tallaght, Dublin 24.

Produced in Ireland by Blackwater Press

Acknowledgements

The author is deeply indebted to all those who have contributed to the writing of this book, in particular to Zoltan Zinn-Collis, Suzi Diamond, Dr Han Collis, Jack Steinberg, Sabina Shorts, Doris Segal, Agnes Bernelle, Rosel Siev, Helen Lewis, Geoffrey Phillips and Joe Briscoe. Without their courage, their kindness and generosity of spirit, this book would not have been possible. Above all else, I wish to acknowledge the fact that for them it had not been easy to come to terms with the past and to speak openly about their memories. I would also like thank Brian Quinn, chairman of the Irish Israeli Fellowship League, Bertha Weingreen, Malvina Harris, Helen McInerney (RTE), as well as the Anti-Defamation League for the use of documents from the Wannsee Conference. I would also like to thank Raphael Siev for granting permission to photograph artefacts from the Jewish Museum in Dublin, and in particular for permission to use the letter of Solly Steinberg and the poem 'The Children of Auschwitz' by Laura Hilman. Special thanks also to Dr Han Collis for her support during the research as well as the kind permission to use photographs and extracts from the books *Straight On* and *The Lost and the Found*; also to Helen Lewis and Blackstaff Press for the permission to use extracts from her book *A Time to Speak*. Many thanks to my agent Jonathan Williams, editor Rachel O'Connor, designer Paula Byrne and photographer Kate Horgan.

Finally, I would like to dedicate *Hidden Memories* to those who have suffered and are still suffering from the Holocaust, as well as to all victims of totalitarianism and ethnic strife throughout the world today.

Contents

Introduction

It could be a sound or a smell. A familiar taste. A photograph in a newspaper. It could be the sound of a dog barking, or a background melody in the supermarket. To an ever smaller number of people, these seemingly innocuous sensations can suddenly trigger off memories of Nazi Germany, bringing back the terror, the pain, and the full force of their grief. For many survivors, as for all those who have been touched by the Holocaust, the burden of their memories has never been fully resolved, often remaining deeply hidden beneath the normal events of everyday life.

In Ireland, there are at least seven people who have had direct experiences of concentration camps during the war. There are many more who have been affected by the Nazi regime, those who escaped but had to leave behind their loved ones – parents, brothers, sisters, cousins, aunts and uncles: relatives and friends whom they never saw again. Some survivors have always felt a duty to preserve the memory of what has become known as the worst crime of the century: the calculated extermination of a race of people. Some survivors have responded to an equally necessary duty to go on living and to try and put the past behind them. Others have been simply unable to talk about the atrocities which they or their families were forced to go through, as though it meant reliving the horror every time.

In this book, many of those I interviewed are speaking for the first time about their fate at the hands of the Nazis. For the 'Belsen children', Zoltan Zinn-Collis and Suzi Diamond, who arrived in Ireland as orphans after the war, the cattle trucks, the starvation, the most inhumane conditions, even the memory of their mothers dying in Belsen, are all indelibly engraved on their childhood minds. Their vivid and fragmented recollections now stand as a tragic and accurate testimony to the death camps. Their stories are echoed by the words of Dr Han Collis, who harboured Jews in Holland during the war and went on to work with the Red Cross in Belsen after its liberation. Along with the well-known Irish physician Dr Robert Collis, she was instrumental in bringing these orphans to Ireland.

Geoffrey Phillips and Rosel Siev both give a moving account of how they were sent away from Germany as children just as the war was beginning, never to see their parents again. Geoffrey Phillips recalls how, along with thousands of other children, he was 13 when he joined the *Kindertransport* (rescue transport for children) and waved goodbye to his mother, carrying only a small suitcase and a bag of provisions. Rosel Siev speaks of how she lost parents, brothers, aunts and uncles; how she was reunited after the war with her sister Hannelore, who was saved by Oscar Schindler, and her sister Hilda, who fled to Palestine. Throughout her life, Rosel hid away all the photographs, unable to discuss these events even with her own children, hoping that the warmth of her home life might help to erase the past which has incessantly haunted her. But as she becomes older, her family's tragedy rises to the surface, more than ever urging her to record the harrowing story. Even as she speaks, she knows she will not sleep.

Helen Lewis recalls how she came through almost three years in the concentration camps, how her career as a dancer kept her alive in Stutthof in Poland, how she became part of one of the notorious death marches and finally saved herself by jumping into a snow-filled ditch to freedom. She recalls how she lost her mother and her husband, how close she came to death herself, and how she remarried and rebuilt her life in Belfast.

Jack Steinberg talks of his newly married sister Ettie leaving her home in Dublin in 1936 to live in Belgium. Two years later, she was taken to the gas-chambers at Auschwitz, along with her husband and two-year-old son while the family in Dublin received nothing but a final heartbreaking postcard. Sabina Shorts and Agnes Bernelle recall the cultural atmosphere of their native Berlin as the Nazis rose to power and drove the Jews out from all areas of society. For Sabina Shorts, whose mother and sister were killed in the Holocaust, a fortuitous escape brought her to Ireland where she encountered the kindness of Irish family life and the benign attitude of Irish officials. Doris Segal talks about leaving her Sudetenland home and coming to the sanctuary of the West of Ireland where her father worked in a Castlebar hat factory, waiting all the time for news of her grandparents, who ultimately died in Auschwitz.

These individual stories of families torn apart and destroyed by Nazi terror are rendered as much as possible in their own words. Since many of those who were adults at the time of World War II are now in their mid-70s at least, this may be the last chance to record their first-hand accounts. At the Anne Frank exhibition in Dublin in 1993, Zoltan Zinn-Collis, who was in Belsen at the same time as Anne Frank, overheard a group of schoolchildren talking in shocked amazement at what had happened in the concentration camps. Zoltan felt compelled to speak to them, telling them that he had been in Belsen. Aghast, they found themselves looking at a survivor of the Holocaust, one of those still alive today who can bear witness to the truth.

Like Zoltan, those who tell their personal and emotional stories here are not pleading for sympathy for themselves. With the passage of time, their accounts have now become a plea for more universal compassion; the Holocaust should not be forgotten and its memory should prevent it happening again to others. Why then, with a half century gone by since the end of the war, are they so concerned that their suffering and the suffering of their families seem often to have been in vain? For many of them, as they hear reports coming from Somalia and Rwanda, Chile, El Salvador and East Timor, even from places as close as Northern

Ireland and Bosnia, there is sometimes little hope. Bereaved families, orphaned children, displaced people, hunger, disease and mass graves; the images are the same.

At the back of the mind lies the uneasy, underlying awareness that this is happening all over again, that the Holocaust victims are merely being replaced by new victims. Everywhere, new families are grieving. And with it comes the ominous feeling that the Holocaust of Nazi Germany was not one finite event, but a part of the cyclical nature of human existence, from which we have not yet rid ourselves. The voices in this book continue to remind us not only of what happened during World War II, but what is happening now. Our inaction can no longer be an excuse to permit others to forsake the basic respect for humanity.

On her visit to Auschwitz in June 1994, President Mary Robinson paid tribute to the victims of Nazi extermination and stressed how important it was not only to remember, but to feel chastened and to remain eternally vigilant. After viewing mounds of human hair, battered suitcases, piles of spectacles, mountains of shoes and photographs of shaven-headed victims going to their death, Mary Robinson remarked that Auschwitz and its horrific time 'is not something that we can say comfortably, it is of the past, it is over'.

It is also important to remember the 20th of July 1944 bomb plot against Hitler for the resistance to the Nazis within Germany. In the airtight, totalitarian state of Nazi Germany, there were those in the *Kreissau Circle* and the *White Rose* who were willing to risk their lives to speak against these crimes. It is important to remember that there were people like Oskar Schindler who harboured Jews. It is essential to remember too, as Helen Lewis testifies in her book *A Time to Speak* that there were good Germans; why not say it? Nobody in this book ever once used the word 'evil'. The crimes of the Holocaust were not committed by 'monsters', as Jennifer Johnston reminds us in her foreword to *A Time to Speak,* but by ordinary people who have been allowed to stray from the path of humanity. Mary Robinson echoes this point by referring to 'the capacity for inhumanity that is within us'.

There is no doubt that films and documentaries, in particular the film *Schindler's List*, have brought the subject of Nazi genocide of the Jewish race to the fore again. In whatever way, the re-creation of these terrible events will undoubtedly spark off the ebbing memories of survivors, our last first-hand link to the truth. Indeed, any attempt at generating an awareness of the subject must be lauded. But with these dramatic accounts, is there not also the possibility that the Holocaust is beginning to fade, bit by bit, into a piece of history? Is it possible that by the next century, the Holocaust will become a nightmarish tale from a forgone century, that it will no longer be a current issue, but a glimpse of the past, written on sand? The survivors and those who lost their loved ones beg us not to betray them and their memories.

Even today, revisionist historians or 'Holocaust deniers' are busy casting doubt on the evidence of planned mass extermination. Their claim is that there is no single proof that the Nazis devised and executed a policy of genocide. The revisionists do not deny that people died in the camps, but they describe the estimated six to twelve million people killed by systematic extermination as a gross exaggeration.

Who can challenge the words of those whose families were removed from their homes and taken away to their death? The fact that from the beginning, through violence and oppression, Nazi ideology won a step by step consensus for their plans to rid Germany of the so-called 'Jewish problem' is not enough. The fact that Hitler saw into the future, long after Jewish extermination, with the remark 'who will remember the North American Indian?' is not enough. The fact that in January 1942 the Wannsee Conference drew up documented plans for what became known as the 'final solution' is not enough. Nor is the fact that when the Nazis were finished with the Jews, they had plans for clearing other non-Aryan races like the Poles and the estimated 30 million Slavs.

Nor is the fact that as rumours of mass killings came back to Germany, many of the commanders in the field called on the Nazi hierarchy to institute more 'refined' measures which would attract less attention.

In physical terms alone, the sheer weight of documentation recording the progress of each Jewish family to the camps still speaks for the dead. The architectural plans for the Auschwitz-Birkenau gas-chambers did not include any water pipes leading to the shower-rooms, confirming that these rooms were conceptually intended for extermination. The plans include many other details, such as a footnote specifying that the doors should be made of 'gas-proof' materials. To this day, you can dip your hand into the 'Pond of Ashes' at Auschwitz and bring up a mass of ash and bone fragments which have not yet disintegrated. There is also the fact that Auschwitz was constructed with transience in mind: huts built with no foundations; the barracks, the crematoria, even the paper which recorded the numbers of people going to their death was very poorly made. Nothing was intended to last. It was all meant to vanish.

But the veracity of all the accumulated evidence never seems to equal the voices of those who witnessed the slaughter with their own eyes. We owe them the right to speak, not only for themselves but also for those who died and have no voice. Their words are underlined by this report from the Irish writer Denis Johnston (*Nine Rivers of Jordan*) who was among the first journalists to arrive in the Buchenwald camp after its liberation:

> As we entered the long hut, the stench hit us in the face, a queer wailing came to our ears. Along both sides of the shed was tier upon tier of what can only be described as shelves. And lying on these, packed tightly side by side, like knives and forks in a drawer, were living creatures – some of them stirring, some of them stiff and silent, but all of them skeletons, with the skin drawn tight over

their bones, with heads bulging and misshapen from emaciation, with burning eyes and sagging jaws. And as we came in, those with the strength to do so turned their heads and gazed at us; and from their lips came that thin, unearthly noise.

Then I realised what it was. It was meant to be cheering...From the shelves feeble arms rose and waved, like twigs in a breeze...

1

Joe Briscoe

Imagine if the Third Reich had extended to Ireland. On 20 January 1942, at the Nazi conference at Wannsee in the north of Berlin, attended by Hitler's top architects of the final solution, Ireland had already been included in the plans for Jewish extermination. Lists had been drawn up of Jewish families: the Abrahamsons, the Solomons, the Goods, the Briscoes. An estimated figure of 4,000 Irish Jews had been included on a now famous Nazi, country by country, draft outline of European Jewry dating from the Wannsee conference.

Naturally, the idea of Nazis arriving in Ireland remains pure hypothesis. But for many people, it may not require a huge leap of the imagination to speculate the shape of Irish history if the Germans had decided to occupy Ireland. Even though, under de Valera's deftly expedient foreign policy, this country remained fiercely neutral throughout the war (de Valera's rather rigid adherence to protocol on the death of Hitler is only further proof of this), it is possible to contemplate enough anti-British feelings remaining for Ireland to have sided with Germany. The Nazis found collaborators in every country in their sweep of Europe, and though the Irish record towards the Jewish race has largely been a tolerant one, with not a single Jew ever losing his or her life because of their faith, there is nothing to suggest that the impact of the Nazis would have been any different from other countries.

Of course there would have been great resistance to the Germans. And it is hard to imagine a country which had been subjected to 800 years of domination, which had only a hundred years previously witnessed millions of Irish people during the Famine dying in coffin ships and through mass starvation, allowing a minority like the Jews among them to be taken away to death camps. And surely some of us, too, would have remembered that the Jews of Russia were among the few who sent donations to Famine relief in Ireland at the time.

But the Irish tolerance for minorities did not extend to allowing Jewish refugees to use Ireland as a sanctuary before or during the war (except for some extraordinary cases). Indeed, James Joyce questioned Irish tolerance by saying that Jews were never persecuted in Ireland, only because 'we never let them in, in the first place'. And with Ireland's fermenting ethnic problems between the Protestant-Catholic divide, who knows what guarantees or favours from the Nazis might have forced the Irish to trade neutrality and principles on humanity. Luckily, many of these questions lie safely in the realm of speculation, but it is essential for Irish people, in order to understand the full significance of the Holocaust in Europe, to place it in an Irish perspective.

Joe Briscoe knows exactly what would have happened if the Germans had come to Ireland. The well-known Dublin Jewish Briscoe family came to live in Ireland from Lithuania in the 1860s and have been prominent in public life. Joe's father, Robert Briscoe was a member of the old IRA and fought in the War of Independence. He took the republican side in the Civil War, was a founder member of the Fianna Fáil party and was elected to the Dáil in 1927. Robert Briscoe became Dublin's first Jewish Lord Mayor in 1956, an honour which was followed by his son, Joe's brother, Ben Briscoe, in 1988. As a teenager in 1945, Joe Briscoe saw newsreels of Belsen at the Carlton cinema and felt a certain detachment. Like many Irish people, he regarded it as something that had happened in Europe and harboured a romantic notion that he would have taken to the hills with his rifle. The Nazis would never have taken him. Now, years later, knowing that 156 European members of his extended family perished in the Holocaust, he feels very different. He understands much more clearly the slow, methodical progression of Jewish extermination.

'If the Nazis had come to Ireland, nothing would have happened at first. After a couple of months, an announcement would be made that food rations could only be collected at the local town hall. I would have gone to Blackrock Town Hall and there would have been a big sign saying: All Jews must state the fact that they are Jews. I had never hidden the fact that I was Jewish. There would have been an Irish Garda standing behind the Nazi officer. I would say my name is Briscoe and they would take a big red stamp and put a J on my card. This would have happened all over Dublin, all over Ireland.'

'Some time later, an announcement would be made on the radio that all Jews were required to go to South Circular Road within forty-eight hours, bringing only those belongings they could carry. So with my handcart, my wife and my little son, we would go there. The houses would be empty and waiting for us. We would be curfewed. Then a wall would have been put up one night at Kelly's Corner and they had you. It's as simple as that. Then the transports would take place. There is no doubt in my mind that the death camps like Auschwitz and Belsen would not have been located here. The Jews would have been taken out of Ireland by boat and rail and ended up somewhere in Europe. That would have been the end of it.'

For a number of years after the war, Joe Briscoe found himself dwelling increasingly on this kind of speculation, believing that Irish Jews were blessed only by the luck of geographic location to have been saved from the calamity. 'One night at three in the morning, I couldn't take this any more. I went into my infant son David's room. He was asleep in his cot. I can remember vividly looking out of the window at the lights around Dublin Bay, and I started to cry. I think these were the bitterest tears I have ever cried. Not for myself but for the agony of these parents who had their young infants dragged from their arms. Here was the light of my life, and to think that something like that could happen was unbearable.'

Joe Briscoe was as yet unaware that any of his extended family had been lost in Europe. Even though he is by nature a relaxed and humorous man, he found himself becoming unreasonably bitter and building up a huge resentment against Germans. As a dentist with a practice in Dublin, Joe Briscoe began to refuse to see German patients. He confronted representatives of the German chemical firm Hoechst and loathed everything German. One day, his postwar hatred of Germans went to such extremes that he broke up Faber Castell pencils he found at home, even though these were made in Cork. 'It was as if I had lit a bonfire in my chest and it got out of control. This hatred was consuming me. My friends saw what was happening to me and told me to forget it.'

It is only when Joe Briscoe met the well-known Danish pastor Paul Borchsenius, who had been involved in the mass transfer of Danish Jews to safety in Sweden during the war, that he was shown how to forgive. 'On no account forget, because if you do it will happen again,' he remembers Paul Borchsenius telling him. But it was important to try and forgive. And it was wrong to inflict the sins of the parents on their children, the young Germans. After a long transition, Joe Briscoe's attitude gradually began to shift and he became far more conciliatory towards Germany in general. In time, his hatred had turned to forgiveness, and he even began to build up a few German patients and friends.

Years later, one Sunday morning, a friend phoned from Carlow to say they had a German visitor with an urgent dental problem. A couple of hours later, he arrived at the dental practice, and as Joe Briscoe began fixing the tooth on his new patient's denture it was revealed that he had lost all his teeth in Russia during the war. Not knowing that he was being treated by a Jew, the patient remarked: 'You have no idea how appalling it was in Russia, Dr Briscoe.' Eventually, when asked what unit of the Wehrmacht he had been attached to, the patient quietly indicated in a conspiratorial whisper that he had been in the SS. An awkward silence fell over the Sunday morning practice as Joe Briscoe chose his words carefully: 'I bet you would never have thought that when you were in the SS in Russia one day a Jew would be fixing your tooth back on your denture,' whereupon the German patient immediately tried to rectify the situation: 'But you don't understand, there were two SSs.'

Joe Briscoe felt it was not his place to make any further remarks over the incident. He refused to charge a fee for the work carried out, saying he had done it for a friend. Having controlled his earlier bitterness towards Germans, he now felt it was not his place to pronounce judgement on any individual in relation to the war. 'I didn't make any smart remarks. And it is interesting that I had no hatred for this man; only pity. The Jews are the most forgiving people in the world, given the unbelievable atrocities and horror they have suffered down through the ages.'

Up until fifteen years ago, Joe Briscoe believed that his family had come through the Nazi period relatively unscathed. On a first trip to Israel, however, he met a distant cousin who had been putting together a family tree. It was only when he counted up the number of entries which had a small Star of David marked beside their names, that he realised how many of his relatives had actually died in the Holocaust.

'All of a sudden you realise that 156 of your uncles, aunts, cousins were all shunted off in cattle carts to their death. But worse was to come. On another visit to Tel Aviv, by chance I met a first cousin of my father's named Tamara Schwalb. Her mother was my father's aunt. After tea and coffee, she turned to me and said: "Joe, I want to ask you a very difficult question. Why didn't your father save my mother's life?"'

Initially, Joe Briscoe had no idea what she was talking about. But she went on to explain how her mother had written to his father, begging him to obtain her an Irish visa to get her out of Berlin. She had managed to get her children away on the famous *Kindertransport* at the time. The British had already closed the borders of Palestine, allowing only a few children in without parents. As a member of the government, and having gone over to Berlin advising Jews to get out of Germany, Robert Briscoe seemed to have been able to do very little to help these fleeing Jews find sanctuary in Ireland. Joe Briscoe's grand-aunt eventually died in the death camps.

'I was absolutely horrified at this news. When I got back to Dublin, I checked the files and it seems these letters had been written. When they released the government documents after the thirty-year embargo, I went through the records and discovered that my father had applied to Gerry Boland, the Minister for Justice at that time, for permits. Gerry Boland had turned him down, saying that he didn't want problems with anti-semitism and the unemployment level was already too high as it was.'

Like their British counterparts, it seems that government officials in Ireland were very reluctant to give refuge to the Jews fleeing the continent at the time. The number of Jewish immigrants allowed into Britain, as into British-ruled Palestine, was kept low. Prime Minister Neville Chamberlain's attitude at the time is summarised by his comment in 1939: 'No doubt the Jews aren't a lovable people; I don't care about them myself, but that is not sufficient to explain the pogrom.' Through extraordinary circumstances, a small number of Jewish refugees did manage to reach Ireland before Germany closed its borders. With hindsight, many will wish to see the reluctance on the part of Irish officials to accommodate the Jews, not so much as an expression of anti-semitic malice, but as a further indication of how few people had envisaged the true outcome of the Nazi nightmare. Whether it was the rigidity of Irish neutrality or the fear of becoming embroiled in European problems, Ireland sealed itself off and the historical records illustrate clearly how official Irish attitudes reacted to their pleas. Although a member of the government of the day, Joe Briscoe's father could do nothing to help his people find refuge here.

'Nobody could possibly have realised what was going to happen. When my father died, my wife and I went through some of his papers and there were many, many letters in German from people begging my father to help them. Letters especially begging to get their children out. They brought tears to our eyes.'

2

Zoltan Zinn-Collis

Zoltan Zinn-Collis has a fear of ESB poles. It's not an irrational fear. They remind him of gallows: the dark, foreboding shapes he has held in the back of his mind since he was four years old. He has a distinct loathing for the song 'Lili Marlene', and he hates the sickly-sweet smell of boiled carrots. At the age of fifty-four, he will not go into a pub because he can't bear physical contact with other people. He cannot join a queue either, because there is something lodged deep in his psyche whereby these things are associated with terror, with grief and loss. He is afraid of being late, with the result that he goes to meetings half an hour, even up to an hour, in advance.

All Zoltan Zinn-Collis's phobias are specifically connected to the Nazi concentration camp at Bergen Belsen, where he was found at the end of the war between the ages of four and five, dying of typhoid and tuberculosis. He had watched his mother die in the arms of his seven-year-old sister, Edith, on the day the camp was liberated in 1945. Before that, their baby sister died on the transport from their Slovakian town in the Tatra mountains of former Czechoslovakia to the camp at Belsen. An older brother, Aladar, died shortly after liberation, leaving Zoltan and his sister on their own, orphans of the Holocaust.

'Whenever I see these ESB poles, I get a shiver because they look just like gallows to me.' His experience echoes the fears which many other survivors still feel to this day – fear of dogs, fear of uniforms, fear of the doorbell ringing, fear of being left without food. Some survivors are known to carry pieces of bread with them whenever they go shopping. Some are obsessed with cleanliness. Others are known to make an instinctive assessment of each new building they enter, seeking out places to hide in case the Holocaust were ever to happen again. Many feel guilty that they are alive while others went to their death.

Zoltan's acute sense of shock at simple everyday things, such as certain vegetables, goes back to the German camps where prisoners were kept barely alive on a staple diet of carrot and turnip water. He is afraid of the sound of shouting, and his fear of being late returns him each time to the early morning roll call in Belsen where they would be severely punished if they were late. These subconscious lesions which compel Zoltan Zinn-Collis to act with a certain caution towards all society, even in the tranquillity of his home life in rural Ireland. His instinctive claustrophobia evokes the cramped conditions which prevailed everywhere on the transport trains and in the concentration camps. And his ingrained, childish fear of queues remains the most eloquent testimony of the endless lines of victims during the Nazi years; queues for food, queues for selection, for delousing, for death.

Zoltan Zinn-Collis lives in Athy and works as a chef at Rathcrogue House just outside Carlow town. Married with four daughters, his life in Ireland has allowed Zoltan to put the past behind him to a great extent. His health still bears the scars of his childhood horror. He is several inches smaller than he should be, has asthma, has had a lung removed and bears a slight deformity in his back from tuberculosis contracted in the camp. However, his robust attitude towards life has enabled him to talk about the circumstances in which he lost his parents and other members of his family. It is when his own daughters ask him where he came from that he feels the difficulties involved in bringing up the subject; it is when his youngest daughter, Emma, is studying the Nazi era at school and comes home to ask his opinion that the past trauma returns most vividly.

It is mostly a fear of loss. He feels the memory of Belsen has left him with a tough protective exterior and a brittle nature. He has tried to interpret these feelings by acknowledging with a certain sadness that he has never really been able to get close to people. 'If you get close to someone, there is a fear of losing them again. When you lose someone at a very early age, you'll be damn careful before you lose someone again. I cannot speak for anyone else, but it's probably that which makes me the loner I am.'

As a survivor, Zoltan has never looked for sympathy, maintaining that excess compassion would actually have made his life harder to live. Indeed, by telling his life story now, facts he has always preferred not to discuss with his own family for fear of straining the relationship with them, he stresses that it is not in order to gain sympathy, but because he feels a duty to speak. It's all happening again, he remarks. He wants to keep the Holocaust in the present tense. Like so many other survivors, he feels guilty for doing nothing.

'Maybe I should have told my children sooner. But I don't think so. I don't want to be somebody special. I just want to be their Dad. I do feel very deeply about what was done to us, in that it was forgotten. If it can be put into context: what was done to me is now being done to others. I feel I need to bear witness. Should I not be shouting from the rooftops?'

On the surface Zoltan lives a normal life, as he says himself, scratching a living in the catering industry, paying his mortgage and his bills. He has a lively, humorous nature, and speaks in a deep voice, tinged with a slight Slovakian or Hungarian accent, though he no longer speaks any of these languages. He describes himself as an Irishman, has never been back to his homeland and feels very much settled in Ireland. On the inside, however, he is very different, because the horror of Belsen will not go away. 'Forgive, absolutely,' he says. 'But never forget.'

Bergen Belsen, in the north of Germany, contained around 500 children when the British tanks entered the camp on 15 April 1945. Originally designed as a transit camp for 5,000 people, Belsen had finally swelled to between 50,000 and 60,000, most of whom were close to death. Of the children found alive, 100 died soon after liberation and two-thirds were badly affected by tuberculosis and typhus. Practically all new born babies died in the first month after birth. Though Belsen camp had never been intended for extermination as such, there were an estimated 23,000 unburied bodies found, most of whom had died of starvation, typhus and dysentery. The stench of Belsen was said to have been picked up as far as twenty miles away.

Deportees who reached Belsen in the latter years of the war would already have had to endure long days, even weeks, in transit in horribly cramped conditions without water, on buses or in rail cars meant for cattle. Of one transport containing 1,000 people, only 200 arrived alive, which meant that being in Belsen alone was already an indication of a will to survive. Zoltan has often felt that his strong instinct for survival, even as a four-year-old child, was not given to his older brother Aladar, who died shortly after liberation. Zoltan's own life was hanging by a thread by the time British troops arrived.

When Zoltan was found, the camp was rife with dysentery. In one of the huts, the floor was six inches deep in faeces in which rows of naked women lay waiting for death. In the worst huts, there would have been 500 people packed together in the final stages of disease. They were starving, covered in lice and had nothing to drink. The last act of the SS before they deserted the camp, fleeing from the advancing Allies, had been to switch off the main water supply.

By the end, the atmosphere in the camp had reached a level of utter insanity, with death and disease all around; there was even evidence of desperate inmates being reduced to cannibalism. Children witnessed scenes of horrific suffering and carnage which is now buried deep in their memories. Indeed, each time I spoke to Zoltan, he recalled vivid new details from his childhood days in Belsen.

Zoltan, his sister Edith and their brother Aladar were found in the camp by Robert Collis, an Irish doctor, and his team, which included his future second wife, Han Collis. After most of the camp survivors had been reunited as much as possible with their own relatives – a difficult task since people hardly recognised the emaciated features of their loved ones – a group of seven children were left with no traceable relatives at all. All these children were brought to Ireland by Dr Collis. Among them were Zoltan and Edith Zinn, Terry Samuels and his sister Suzi (now Suzi Diamond), Evelin Schwartz, who was adopted in Dublin and emigrated to Australia with her new family, as well as two other boys who went to orphanages in Northern Ireland. Terry and Suzi were adopted into the Samuels family, while Zoltan and Edith were adopted into the Collis family and lived in Fitzwilliam Square, Dublin, where Robert Collis had his medical practice.

'Every now and again there is a TV programme on the Holocaust and you see piles of bodies and I look at those and I say which one of those was my father? Is that my mother on the top, right there, under that pile? I wonder what kind of a life I would have had normally if this hadn't happened,' Zoltan said on an RTE radio documentary with Helen McInerney.

Zoltan considers that his childhood was taken from him and that his life really began only when he was nine or ten years old. He feels his rehabilitation is due in part to the great influence of Newtown, the Quaker school he attended in County Waterford. It is only now, when he looks around him and observes the lives of his own children that he comes face to face with his own loss. When Zoltan got married, there was only one member of his family present among the thirty-four wedding guests. It is when

Zoltan's daughters want to know about his background that he discovers how empty that part of his life is and how, in effect, half a family is missing.

'Why are my eyes filling up?' Zoltan asks. 'The last time I went to a concert everybody was having such a good time that I started to cry. This is a physical reaction, when people are together enjoying themselves. When I used to take my daughters up to Funderland on their birthday, it would have the same effect. Just looking at children being children, having a good time and I being responsible for it. It's probably because I don't remember much of that myself, that feeling of not having a care in the world.'

Speaking to Zoltan, you come away with a strong impression of a well-adjusted person, settled in Athy with all the privileges of a happy life. But the questions he occasionally asks about his own life uncover the stolen innocence of his childhood. 'You wouldn't think anything has happened to me. But what sort of person would I have been without that background? I have already said that I find personal relationships difficult. Is it on account of what happened to me in the past? It's difficult to speak about it without appearing to be looking for sympathy, or without making yourself out to be a great guy for having survived. I don't want to come over as – oh, poor me, look what's been done to me. Of course, maybe I'm overcompensating. I don't know, but I do think that history must have something to do with it.'

Zoltan does not regard himself as a social being and feels that his body language is protective, keeping people from coming too close.' I don't like going into pubs. I don't like physical contact, standing at the bar with somebody coming up to you and throwing his arms around you. It's not me at all.'

At times, in order to piece his life together and to come to terms with the random chance by which he has survived and is now living at such a remote distance to those places of horror, Zoltan often wonders what relevance the Holocaust has today.

People in Ireland see it as such a distant thing. When he talks to neighbours, he realises that few of them know his story or what he has gone through.

'I live in a cul de sac with twenty-two houses. We all know each other. The kids play together. We all look after each other. There isn't a house where I wouldn't feel free to walk in the back door. I sometimes try to equate the whole thing to my own neighbours. I say "look, take that family down there. They're the same as my family; mother, father and four children. Some day for some reason, someone doesn't like the colour of their eyes or their hair and decides to take them away and dispose of them. That is what happened to us." '

Zoltan maintains that the only way to present the evidence of extermination during the Nazi regime to new generations is to personalise it. He is of the opinion that television and film serve only to remove it from reality, that we have already become immune to the same thing happening again in our own time. 'When they bring up these pictures of the Holocaust, or make a film like *Schindler's List*, it's entertainment. 'I think it should be brought through to young people that it was reality, so that they realise that this actually happened. How many people in Ireland know that somebody like me exists? How many of us survivors are there in Ireland and how many of us are left worldwide? When we are gone, who is going to speak for us? This is why I think that I've got to talk about it now. I survived and I think I owe it to those people who didn't.' Until a few years ago, the idea of opening himself up to a stranger and talking about his past life would have horrified Zoltan. Now he feels he has a duty to speak, not merely for himself and his own family but for all the others who perished.

'I remember the barracks or the huts, or whatever we lived in. I remember the rows of bunks, three tier. I remember we were in the middle barracks, in the middle bunk, with somebody above and somebody below. The ones above were not very nice, I don't know why, and the ones below were OK. I remember the morning roll call; we all had to troop out in the cold, it would have been bloody cold. I remember all the mothers telling the children to be quiet and stay still, because if you didn't you were likely to be disposed of. I remember running up and down the barracks, chasing other kids, I don't even know who they were. During morning roll call, the adults sang, 'Lili Marlene'. Way back here in my mind there is that memory, and I get an uneasy feeling whenever I hear the song.

'I vaguely remember the liberation. I know we were liberated on the day my mother died. I don't even know her name. There were many survivors who made it physically but not mentally. My sister was three or four years older than I am. I have a vague memory of my mother dying. My sister went to try and get some water, my brother was also alive at the time. And she came back without any water, saying in effect we were free. She went over to my mother and my mother literally died in her arms then. So if you are seven or eight years old and your mother is dead in your arms with your two younger brothers beside you, it's going to do something to you sometime.'

Who knows to any accurate degree what scars were left behind by exposure to such horror at a young age? Indeed, Zoltan is still vividly aware of the effects of Belsen today, and though many of the tragic events he witnessed as a child are buried beyond retrieval in his memory, he still very much recalls the terror, the degradation and the huge sense of loss which goes back to the Nazi years. Joyce Barcroft, a voluntary worker at Fairy Hill Hospital in Howth where Zoltan and Edith, along with the other children of Belsen, were brought, spoke in an RTE documentary about Zoltan's earliest memories as a child, still in bed recovering from tuberculosis. She would read picture books to the children and, on one occasion, Zoltan pointed out a cat and said they had once had a cat at home. Then they were taken away.

'Once he [Zoltan] told me that they were made to stand outside in the cold and he had been hidden under a pile of bodies at night-time, so that he wouldn't be found. To live with those memories must be appalling. It was hard to realise just how bad it was, because he never said he was suffering. All he would say sometimes is that they were very cruel to him, but they didn't mean to be. I think he had been taught that during his time in Sweden [where the children were initially brought for a brief period after Belsen], so that he wouldn't feel badly about it.'

3

Zoltan and Edith

Zoltan Zinn-Collis was born in August 1940 in the foothills of the Tatra mountains in former Czechoslovakia, not far from the village of Gerlachov. His father, Adolf, was a Slovakian Jew, his mother a Hungarian whose cultured family descended from the Zip Germans of Slovakia. Though many of the Zip Germans stood to gain from the invasion of Czechoslovakia, his mother's family despised the Nazi ideology and gave their blessing to the marriage of their daughter to Adolf Zinn.

The young Zinn family lived in a modest three-roomed cottage, surrounded by forests and mountains. Zoltan recalls the back-yard at home, the wall and the outside tap. He recalls his toy trumpet which he used to fill with water in the hope that it would make a new sound. There was an outside toilet with a wooden door and an uncle once shot a hole through the door with a hunting gun. 'I have another scene in my mind of being sent off to school one day with my sister Edith. There were lines and lines of artillery pieces. I thought this was fantastic; little boys and guns, you know. And then I remember going to school with Edith and sitting behind her and being shown how to fold my arms and going home and saying "Look, I can fold my arms. Wow". I remember my father as a tall man with a moustache. My mother was a small woman. I can't remember her name, or my baby sister's name.'

The children were brought up with three languages: Czech, Hungarian and German. In order to protect them from the dark threat to the Jewish race at the time, they were baptised into the Reformed Church and, like their mother, never had any connections with the Jewish religion other than by marriage. To this day, Zoltan has never been into a synagogue and only in a very broad sense describes himself as a Christian.

But the fact that his father, Adolf Zinn, was a Jew, would be enough eventually to condemn them all to the long agonising journey to the concentration camps. A Slovak by birth, Adolf eked out a modest living as a painter and decorator until he fell on hard times and came to the attention of the SS. During the purges of Slovakian Jews which went on relentlessly into the latter years of German occupation, Zoltan's father was inevitably forced to go into hiding in the forests around their home. The children remember him coming back to the house from time to time, ragged, dishevelled and hungry. 'I remember us all sitting around the table eating bread with sugar, except that my father always had salt and pepper on his.'

There were an estimated 140,000 Jews in Slovakia at the beginning of the war. Most of these had done particularly well, so much so that they were envied by Slovakian peasants, who were quick to seize the opportunity of Hitler's reign to point them out for transportation and to take over their homes and belongings. It has always been impossible to understand the logic of these purges towards the end of the war, since the German army was already facing defeat, with the Russian armies only a few weeks away, and the Slovak regime crumbling. But instead of conserving their resources and concentrating on defence, the Nazis in Slovakia, as well as other areas to the east, intensified the efficiency of their extermination programme, rounding up any remaining Jews and, in the end, using much-needed transport to send them to camps inside Germany; Belsen, for instance, was one of the furthest camps from Slovakia. During these years, over 120,000 Jews were transported to Poland or Germany, where most of them were exterminated.

While her husband was in hiding, Zoltan's mother continued to fend for herself and her children as best she could with the help of her relatives. For a while they went about unhindered by the Nazi *Einsatzgruppen* in the locality. But her marriage to a Jew was widely known and was eventually pointed out to a German officer, who then came to the house to try and persuade her to renounce her marriage. Armed soldiers searched the house and the officer referred to her good Hungarian stock, saying that it was not too late to rectify the mistake. The Führer would acknowledge her Aryan background. All she needed to do was to present herself at the local town hall the following day, sign her name and her marriage would be annulled.

Adolf Zinn's wife stood by her husband and announced that her love for him could not allow her to go along with these terms. After a further, polite attempt to convince her, the officer left, indicating that her defiance of the Third Reich directives would bring trouble. With this new threat, the family devised a scheme whereby a Hungarian uncle would vacate his house for the Zinn family. The important thing for them was not to be seen about the neighbourhood and to remain indoors. But after some time in hiding, Adolf, who had spent months out in the open, became claustrophobic and sought out a local hostelry where he was spotted and betrayed to the Germans.

When the Nazi raiding party arrived, he was beaten and forced to say where his family was hiding. They were all brought to a barracks where they were joined by their former neighbours, Mrs Holländer and her daughter, Anna. Many of the details around the transportation to Belsen and the death of Zoltan's mother were recorded first hand by Dr Robert Collis (*The Lost and the*

Found) from his conversations with Edith Zinn-Collis, who now lives in county Wicklow, as well as with Mrs Holländer, who survived Belsen to tell the story of the Zinn family. Zoltan has never questioned his mother's decision to remain loyal to his father. All over the Third Reich, families like these had stood by their Jewish partners as they went to work camps, not for one moment imagining that they were going to their doom.

The following morning both families, along with many others, were herded towards the railway station and onto cattle trucks. In the confusion, surrounded by random gunfire, the Zinns lost their suitcase and all their belongings. Adolf Zinn became separated from his wife. As the tortuous journey went on for six days through the midwinter cold, the greatest fear was that there would not be enough milk to feed the baby. There were so many people packed into the truck that it was impossible for more than a few to sit down at one time. In an effort to keep order inside the cattle truck, one woman took control and after battling with all the different languages, managed to divide the occupants into four, with one quarter sitting down at a time. But the descending chaos in this confined space had already begun to reach a hysterical level with no food provided all day, with only one cup of water each, and the train stopping only every six hours to allow people to get out and relieve themselves.

The children became very hungry and cried continuously. A whole day went by before the train stopped and they were eventually given turnip and potato soup. Since there was still no milk for the baby, Zoltan's mother was forced to give her soup and breadcrumbs which made her very ill. Many people contracted severe diarrhoea because of the soup, and the stench in the boxcar became unbearable.

When the train stopped the following day and the guards had still not let people out, some young girls managed to push the door open and slip out to crouch down on the embankment. To the horror of the people watching from inside the boxcar, a guard who spotted the girls shot one of them who was trying to flee and whipped the others back onto the train. The truck door was then secured with ropes and kept sealed. For four days and nights without food or water, they lurched from town to town, setting up agonising cries of despair.

From here on, the fate of this tightly packed crowd of women and children reached a frenzy of torment. Women clawed each other, collapsed, were trampled on and died. The Zinns and Holländers huddled together in a corner where they had to fight for their children's lives. A crazed old woman kept reaching out to Zoltan saying that she would put him out of his pain, and Mrs Holländer's daughter was seized by two other women from whom she had to be dragged back. At first, all the children wailed, but then became ominously quiet. The baby, who had vomited for two days, dropped her head back and died. When the cattle truck eventually stopped, only those who were still alive got out, leaving behind the dead bodies, which were piled up on the platform. Zoltan's mother was still carrying her dead baby in her arms and gave it up only when she was commanded to do so by a German officer. When they were finally given water and milk, she set about reviving the remaining children, Edith, Aladar and Zoltan.

In the selection process which ensued on the platform, wives and husbands met briefly, only to be separated again when it was deemed that most of the healthy would be sent for forced labour while the old, the sick and the very young were sent directly for extermination. Being under five, Zoltan would have been destined for the crematorium only for the fact that his mother lied to a guard and insisted that he was over five and that he was not a Jew. Elsewhere, there are harrowing stories recorded of how children falsified their age in order to be placed in work camps, only to be laughed at by the SS in these selection procedures. Zoltan's father was taken away to Sachsenhausen and they never saw him again. For a few weeks, both the Zinn and Holländer families stayed in Ravensbrueck transit camp, where they were deloused, had their heads shaved, were given blue-striped pyjamas and held in filthy huts infested with fleas and lice. They had to struggle each day for their food. The camp also held many distraught children who had come back from Auschwitz without their parents.

The transport onwards to Belsen was by bus, a vehicle which was packed with sixty Dutch orphans along with the Zinns and the Holländers. Zoltan recalls the mud and the headlights of the bus in the night. Very soon, this bus, which had to evade the nightly bombing raids of allies, became a further source of terror, with a whole German town razed to the ground beside them. The journey, which lasted over two days, took on the same features as the cattle truck, with children suffering diarrhoea and hunger apace. When they arrived in Belsen, there was snow on the ground and the first thing that confronted them were the corpses of inmates who had died overnight and had not yet been taken away. Day by day, more and more people began to arrive from camps in the east which were being evacuated ahead of the advancing Russian armies.

Belsen was constructed in the middle of a dense forest, surrounded by watchtowers and barbed wire fences, men separated from women and children into two quarters. Children learned very soon that approaching one of the fences would mean the risk of being shot from one of the watchtowers. To avoid typhus spreading to any of the surrounding German villages, the guards were instructed to shoot any escapers on sight. The struggle to remain alive in this camp was such that, in desperation, many inmates actually committed suicide by running at the fences. By early 1945, the overcrowding drove inmates to insanity. There were no toilet or washing facilities. There was no privacy, and the filthy conditions assisted the spread of fever throughout the camp.

At first the dead were collected each morning and were cremated or buried, but as time went by and the German armies were gradually but steadily defeated by the advancing Russians in the east and the British and Americans in the south and on the western front, the camp was virtually left to fend for itself and the daily piles of corpses were simply left to decompose in the open. Again the fear of typhus stopped the guards from approaching the huts except when necessary, delivering the thin soup and withdrawing immediately.

Though many were forced to fight in order to stay alive, the women and children were said to be less exposed to the kind of violence which had become widespread among the male prisoners at the camp. Zoltan's mother managed to feed her children to some extent through the bizarre compassion of a female SS officer named Schwarz. The prisoners were terrified of her, but their mother was so desperate that she begged this woman for a little food; her boys Zoltan and Aladar already had typhus. Without saying a word and at risk to herself, SS officer Schwarz each day smuggled in a little bread and milk to the Zinn family. Even when she was caught out and punished, this officer continued to single them out for help.

But then the worst thing of all happened when Zoltan's mother contracted typhus. Edith, the only one without fever, became the sole provider. Each day, in going out to look for water, she was soon confronted with the true horrors of Belsen. She watched people being murdered, people being flogged, and people dying in agony. She saw children like herself coughing up blood without stopping before they gave up and died. Soon she became immune to the sight of dead bodies all around and devoted herself to caring only for her mother and brothers.

All this inevitably took its toll on Edith as she struggled with these memories later in life. Surviving the physical conditions of this camp may have been one thing, but the survival of a child growing up with these horrific memories is another entirely. For a child of seven to be plunged into adulthood and forced to fight for the life of her family demanded heroic qualities. Dr Robert

Collis, who later brought Edith and Zoltan to Ireland, concluded that her mother had imparted some of her extraordinary strength to her daughter.

By April 1945 there were rumours running through the camp that the British forces were not far away, giving the camp inmates a new sense of hope, only to be denied that optimism again when bombs hit the water supply instead of the German *Wehrmacht* barracks up the road. The camp was thrown into further chaos with renewed escape attempts in which many were shot down. Largely abandoned to their own lot, crazed mobs of prisoners roamed through the camp, stealing from the dying, fighting among themselves and sending further waves of delirium and terror through the densely packed huts. Towards the end, bread was received only once a week and soup or gruel three times a week. As the Germans eventually began to abandon the camp, leaving the Hungarian SS in charge, their last vicious act was to switch off the water supply and leave the already starving and emaciated occupants to their own fate. For the last six weeks in Belsen, there was no water supply and no electricity, and the inmates desperately burst open pipes, climbing over bodies and dodging the shots of the Hungarian SS in order to reach a small trickle flowing from the main pump. It was the hottest April in years and people died for lack of water.

On 15 April 1945, the British army finally arrived at Belsen and liberated the camp. One of the last things which Zoltan's mother heard was the sound of cheers going up all around her: 'We're free, the war is over, the Germans are beaten.' But all this came too late for her and, in the arms of her seven-year-old daughter Edith, she finally succumbed to the fever and died. The last thing she said to Edith was to look after the boys and never to become separated from them.

4

Han Collis

To this day, Han Collis still vividly recalls the impact of going into Belsen where she worked with a team of nurses under Dr Robert Collis. At her home in Newtownmountkennedy, Co. Wicklow, the Dutch-born doctor, who had harboured Jewish refugees during the war in Holland, remembers the confusion and panic at the enormous scale of the tragedy at the camp where 800 people continued to die by the day for weeks after liberation. She recalls thinking how much more they could have done with greater numbers of medical volunteers, how they had to choose between the sick and the hopeless, and how they celebrated the first day, four weeks after her arrival in May, when the daily death toll had been reduced to 300.

'It took us about two days to get there, and when we got to Celle, which was twenty miles away from Belsen, we very soon realised we were in concentration camp land. There was barbed wire with the skull and crossbones signs warning against typhus. Then the smell of 23,000 corpses hit us. It was unbelievable; there were thousands and thousands of corpses lying around and it was a warm summer. The dead and the dying were mixed up. When you went into the barracks, you had to be very quiet. At the bottom of five corpses, you might hear a soft clapping, very very faint, and you would know that someone was alive and that this was the only way they could draw attention to themselves.'

At the time, Han (Hogerzeil) Collis was a law student who had taken part in the Dutch underground operations, concealing three Jewish families from deportation by sharing responsibility for a house in which they lived under a false identity. 'The Jewish ladies I was hiding in the house were very funny. The Jewish sense of humour is marvellous. We'd open the fire of the stove and tell stories, real Yiddisher stories. We would be in tears of laughter. I didn't know any of the identities of these women because they had false names. One of the women had a four-year-old daughter living not far away and was unable to make any contact with her; even when they passed in the street they had to ignore each other. They both survived. Later on towards the end of the war, we could not even let our Jewish women outside, and eventually when things began to get a bit hot, we had to split them up and I went south to Tilburg.'

People sold the doors of their house for bread. They ate tulip bulbs which made them very sick. Forbidden to own a radio, Han Collis hid their radio, wrapped in a rubber bag, in a cesspit at a farm at the back of the house. They would have been shot if they had been caught listening to the BBC every night at 9 p.m. Han recalls how the attitude of German friends changed over the years as the Hitler regime began to tighten its grip on Europe.

'It was a very insidious process. My mother went to school with a German girl in Switzerland in the early 30s and every year got a letter from her. One year her friend wrote about this man Hitler whom she thought was mad and that everything possible should be done to make sure that he was stopped. The following year her friend sent a Christmas letter saying that things really weren't that bad after all. The year after was 1935 and my mother's friend wrote again saying that everything in Germany was working out wonderfully well; her children were having a great time in the Hitler Youth, and anyway "it was such a mess with all those foreigners here, I'm glad something is being done about them."'

The fact that Han Collis had managed to learn Yiddish over the years of occupation, as well as several other languages, gave her a very prominent role in the aftermath of liberation where she could communicate easily with the survivors at Belsen and the relief workers from many other countries. She had joined the Red Cross at Tilburg, and shortly afterwards met Dr Robert Collis, who had arrived with the British Army Red Cross initially to investigate how bad things had been in Holland, only to find out that the situation was far worse in the German camps.

'At that point all that we knew was that the Jews had been taken away to work for the new Germany. And because they never came back, people began to talk in a whisper and say "I wonder what this is. The last time I saw my mother is when she went off on that bus three years ago and I know she would have contacted me." We knew that something had gone wrong; something horrible had happened. But how could you imagine anything like Belsen? It was only on the morning that Bob Collis arrived that we saw a newspaper photograph of stacks and stacks and stacks of bodies.'

Arriving in Belsen was worse than anything she could have imagined. At the same time, Han recalls a very positive atmosphere among the relief workers. The atrocities under Nazi Germany were beyond words and the world was just beginning to grasp the newly discovered concept of 'death camp' in all its horror. Finally, after living under German occupation and seeing many of her friends disappear and go to their death, she saw that something could be done. Han Collis trained to be a doctor only after the war, but volunteered to do whatever she could at the time; making sheets, scrubbing floors and nursing the sick back to health.

'The thing that moved me more than anything else was this huge pile of shoes. Shoes are somehow part of you and your personality. You see tiny little children's shoes, and high-heeled shoes, and half-broken old men's shoes. For me that was the very worst. In fact it was worse than seeing a dead person. These people had put on these shoes and possibly walked to their death in them.'

Bergen Belsen was soon dubbed the 'horror camp' and medical corps were able to do very little except to bury the dead and set up some kind of primitive recovery unit. They had very little food and because typhus was spread by lice, they had to wash everyone and delouse them, a major operation in itself which proved too much for many of the infirm. There was little discipline and many of the survivors instinctively hoarded food and blankets so that it took weeks before any order could be established. Among these thousands of skeletal shapes, there seemed to be no difference between men and women, and relatives often failed to recognise each other.

In Belsen, as in many other concentration camps, the allied soldiers entering and seeing the carnage instantly turned their rage on the remaining SS camp guards, beating them, forcing them to bury the dead, feeding them on rations which the prisoners had received up to then. In some of the camps, former prisoners with enough strength left also vented their anger and killed their tormentors. In Dachau, for instance, camp guards disguising themselves in prisoners' pyjamas were easily spotted because of their healthy faces and well-fed bodies. In Belsen, some of the SS men, killed by the fists of angry liberating soldiers, ended up being buried in enormous pits along with the mass of corpses; some begged to be shot, though this was not granted. Others caught typhus from handling the dead, but they were not treated as patients like their victims.

Half a mile away from Belsen, there was a German military training compound, as well as a fully equipped hospital with X-ray rooms, operating theatres and laboratories. The first task in Belsen was purely a sanitary one, clearing the dead and making sure that disease did not spread beyond the camp. Military authorities were faced with the job of removing everybody into improvised hospital quarters at the German army compound nearby, a massive undertaking which would take weeks. An SOS had been sent out and medical students, doctors and nurses began to arrive.

Initially, things were slow to improve for the most vulnerable at Belsen. For Zoltan, Edith and Aladar, now alone after their mother's death, the conditions changed only gradually at first. SS men, driven by British soldiers at gunpoint, came into the barracks and took their mother away to be flung on a cart and buried in a mass grave. The children received hot milk with sugar and white bread which only made them sick. Days went by without any nursing care. With the two boys now seriously ill and too weak even to eat the food which was brought every day, their lives hung in the balance.

One morning, Dr Robert Collis arrived at the camp to set up a special ward, changing the fate of the 500 children left alive. A half circle of large army tents were set up outside the new quarters for these young patients. Zoltan, who was very ill with typhus and tuberculosis, remembers other children running in and out under the flaps of the tents. His older brother did not survive, however, having gone into a coma, he was beyond medical help. Edith, who ran a slight temperature, was soon moved into what was known as the 'well block'.

In Nazi-occupied Europe, the pre-war Jewish child population came to about 1.6 million. During the war, an estimated 1.5 million were killed, leaving only six to seven per cent alive by 1945. The fact that the adult Jewish population under the Reich survived at a higher rate of 33 per cent points to the fact that, under the Nazi extermination plans, Jewish children had always been a special target. For the generations in between, sterilisation programmes had been set up, at Auschwitz – Birkenau under Joseph Mengele primarily, and though these operations with the crude use of X-Ray and barium were nothing but barbaric, the intention was obviously to stop the proliferation of the Jewish race, while at the same time keeping the healthiest adults for work programmes to support the Reich.

Upon reaching the extermination camps, most children were sent to their death. In general, all children under twelve, as well as all people over forty-five, were killed. Every now and then, a healthy child who looked older would slip through the system. For instance, in one French roundup of Jews in July 1942 in which 9,000 people were sent to Auschwitz, 4,000 of whom were children, only thirty people returned home after the war, none of them children. Most of the children who survived the Holocaust were hidden in attics, huts, cupboards, sewers and in the wild. Some of them posed as Catholics, outwardly renouncing their faith. Some were concealed in convents. Jews also sent their offspring to safety on the *Kindertransport*, where trains full of children were sent abroad before the German borders were closed. Many of these became orphaned as their parents and relatives died in the death camps.

Among the orphans found in Belsen were Terry and Suzi (Tibor and Zsuszi Molnar) Samuels, who had come from a Jewish Hungarian background. Their family had been killed. All that is known is that in one weekend, 25,000 Hungarian Jews were murdered together. In May 1945 Suzi would have been just under two years of age and only barely alive. Her five-year-old brother Terry was well and is remembered by Han Collis, feeding and caring for his baby sister Suzi, who had typhus. When it emerged that Terry and Suzi, along with Zoltan and Edith and another German Jewish orphan named Evelin Schwarz, had no traceable relatives, Dr Collis undertook to bring them all back to Ireland and find parents who would adopt them.

Han Collis recalls how she translated Zoltan's first words in German. As he began to recover, he held Robert Collis's hand and said in German: 'My father is dead, now the doctor is my father.' It was then that Dr Collis made the decision to adopt Zoltan and Edith. Though they never actually became legally adopted under Irish law, which demanded that the adoptive parents had to be of the same religion, they were brought up in Dublin by the Collis family.

As soon as they turned the corner and came out of the crisis of their illness, many of the survivors began to recover very quickly, putting on weight on a daily basis. Food began to arrive in greater supply. A consignment of Red Cross parcels destined for POWs, which had been held up during the last months of the war, had been found in German ports. They had come from England, America and Canada and included extracted butter and jam, Canadian milk, lemon curd, orange juice, as well as fine cheeses, soup, biscuits, creamed rice and pineapple.

In the book *Straight On*, co-written by Robert Collis and Han Hogerzeil, they record the moment where the immediate physical threat to the children of Belsen began to subside.

> Dinner time was now like feeding time... children waited breathlessly in bed and waved their spoons. One put on as much as ten pounds in one week! And as they ate they became happy and laughter filled the place. The terror vanished in conscious form and they seemed altogether happy on the surface. People seeing them then said that of all the people the children had suffered least mentally, but later we found Gunther Goldbroch drawing the Long Gallows at Lublin in a book and another little Dutch boy, aged five, was heard to say when asked where he had last seen his father, 'hanging by his tie from the door'. Who therefore will say how these children will behave in later life, what images of terror they will have hidden in their subconscious minds...
>
> *Straight On* (1947)

Next to the urgent food requirements, clothing became the most immediate necessity. Han recalls how the striped prison pyjamas had to be incinerated because of lice infestation and how big a problem it was to find clothes for over 20,000 people at once. 'We requisitioned clothes in shops and houses, and stuffed them into this huge shed which we called Harrods. They came in wearing striped pyjamas or draped in blankets and came out on the other side clean and dressed, and looking normal to a certain extent. This gave them great dignity. We also had a make-up table where the women put on lipstick and powder.'

At the same time, Han recalls how funny and slightly ridiculous the whole episode sometimes seemed. 'It had its hilarious side too. And it's always very easy to have a laugh with Jewish people because they're so witty.' For some people who could not believe their luck, this sudden amelioration became overpowering and many began to steal and hoard everything they could get their hands on. They filled their quarters with trinkets, cushions and dolls. One woman was found hiding seventeen dresses.

In their book Robert Collis and Han Hogerzeil recall a dance organised for recovering internees which took place in one of the squares between the blocks, where green trees had been planted and coloured lights were strung up between the flagpoles.

The girls came dressed in their new finery. Some could hardly walk, others looked as if they'd break in two. The music started and the dance began. Each British soldier took a girl and swung her on his arm. The tanned brown faces of the soldiers showed up strangely against the pallor of many of those with whom they danced. One very tall young Canadian Airforce sergeant danced with a tiny girl who came up only to his waist, holding her in his huge arms as he waltzed around with a great smile upon his boyish face.

Straight On (1947)

5

Suzi Diamond

Suzi Diamond remembers the trains and the cattle trucks. She remembers people coughing, people being tortured, the bright red Nazi flag flying over Belsen. She remembers being hosed down with water. She remembers the big house where she came from in Hungary, the photograph of her father, the first taste of chocolate after liberation.

For the past fifty years, since Suzi (Molnar/Samuels) Diamond was brought to Ireland from Belsen at the age of two by Dr Robert Collis, it has always been much easier for her to say nothing and leave the memory of Belsen to her older brother Terry, who also lives in Dublin. Terry Samuels's recollection of life as a child in Belsen is perhaps one of the better-known Irish accounts of those times. Now, after seeing the film *Schindler's List* and looking back over the evidence of the Nazi years, Suzi has decided to speak for the first time about her own strong, hidden memories of these events.

Suzi Diamond lives in the Dublin suburb of Clonskeagh. She feels compelled to talk about her past which has remained submerged until now. When I spoke to her, she felt as though her memory as a two-year-old in Belsen has been discounted, that it was always assumed that she would have remembered nothing and that she survived the horror unaffected by the psychological scars which many Holocaust victims carry with them.

Adopted by Willie and Elsie Samuels, an Orthodox Jewish family who owned a well-known jewellery shop on Grafton Street, Suzi was brought up in Palmerstown with her brother Terry, who is five years older. She went to school in Alexandra College and, at the age of twenty, married solicitor Alec Diamond. They have two grown up children. While her adoptive mother was still alive, Suzi always obeyed an unspoken obligation to live a full and happy life in Ireland where the destruction of her natural family at the hands of the Nazis would never be discussed.

It is as though she had two lives: one that disappeared and another which began with her arrival in Ireland. Only now can she put past and present together in any coherent way. She does not know her mother's or her father's names. All that remains from the past are a passport with her thumbprint signature and some vivid and shocking flash memories which keep recurring throughout her life and which have been triggered off more recently by TV documentaries about the Third Reich.

'I remember more than I think I remember, if that sounds feasible. I was looking at a photo taken in the rehabilitation camp after the war which Han has in her possession. I wasn't in the photo myself but I recognised the place and said to her – oh yes, to the right, out of the picture, that's where the fence was and where we used to play. Han said: "You are quite right." So I do remember. I don't remember where we came from or where we were going to, only that we came from Hungary [Debrecen, north-east of Budapest] and that we went to Belsen obviously. All that I remember is a big house at home, and I remember a photograph of my father. My mother used to say: "That's your father," so that I would remember him. My brother says that my father thought he was joining the army, but it was one of these scams to lure him out.

'We don't remember when the knock came on the door. But I remember walking; I must have been an early walker. And I do remember the train; the long, oblong-shaped carriage. My mother went over to one of the corners; there were no seats, only wooden floors, and the three of us huddled together. An old lady sat diagonally opposite us with a shawl and she was coughing and coughing, driving everyone mad. All the others were moaning and groaning and she was coughing. Eventually she stopped and I thought – "great, she's stopped coughing at long last". I thought no more about it.

'At some stage my brother wanted to go to the toilet and my mother lifted him up to these slits, which was where the air came through. [He actually stood on his mother's shoulders and relieved himself through an air vent in the cattle truck.] And eventually I wanted to go too. There were two big buckets provided as toilet facilities and they were getting fuller and fuller and, as you can imagine, the smell was getting worse. When I had to go, didn't the train jerk and the whole thing go all over me. It really was awful and I remember my mother taking my clothes off and trying to hang them somewhere to dry.'

Suzi recalls getting off the train, the rush of people trying to scramble out of the rail car and her mother staying behind with the two of them until everyone else had got out. 'I remember seeing the old lady who had been coughing all the time and saying to my mother: why isn't she getting off? I didn't realise she was dead. Not until years later, it dawned on me.'

On arrival at Belsen, Suzi, her brother and her mother went through the terrifying ordeal of being washed down and deloused with powerful hoses. Fifty years later, she still cannot take a shower because it brings back horrific memories lodged at the back of her mind in those formative childhood years. As the camp guards turned the hoses on them, she was held under her mother's arm while her brother Terry was held tightly in her mother's other hand. In an effort to retain possession of a tiny piece of soap, her mother asked Terry to stick it to the back of her leg, but the soap fell off and disappeared. Even now, the impression on Suzi of water being associated with terror as part of a huge violent act goes back to the sense of utter chaos among the frightened crowds in the delousing tunnels. 'To this day I hate getting water over my eyes or face, because it was terrifying – all this water gushing at you. I swim alright, but I'll never put my head under water. I hate to be splashed and I'll always have a bath by choice instead of a shower.'

At Belsen, the children were at times relatively free to move around. Suzi, her brother and their mother were housed close to the entrance of one of the huts which had a concrete floor. Suzi was soon taught never to discard anything that might be useful; bits of food, scraps of paper, all the things a child might find along the floor of the huts. Suzi also remembers the filth of their living quarters and how her brother once witnessed a man falling into the latrines and drowning there. Most of the old and infirm were held as they crouched backwards over the latrine which was the size of a swimming pool. But in this case, a rather weak and starving man on his own fell backwards and, while the camp guards jeered at him, drowned in the sea of urine and faeces.

'I never go into a public toilet; it's a very sensitive thing. I am also a compulsive cleaner, and my husband is always reminding me that the bathroom doesn't have to be cleaned every day. But I can't stand the idea of anything not being clean and I feel this is definitely a reaction to the filth of the camps.' Suzi also gets moments of claustrophobia and has found herself walking out of restaurants where there was lots of noise or where the ceiling was very low.

Like many Hungarian children, Suzi had her ears pierced and wore gold sleepers which had been given to her by her father. 'They took away my gold earrings and I was very upset. I remember my mother saying: "Don't cry, we'll buy you some more." Later on, my adoptive parents, who owned a jewellery shop, kept encouraging me to get my ears pierced, but I couldn't. It's only very recently that I've started to wear earrings again.

'I remember my mother quite well. She was small, I remember her being thin, but I don't know if that was because she was in the camps or because she was naturally that way. She had black hair. Short hair. I don't know her name, nor my father's first name. I remember her giving us some of her rations and she gave me more than my brother. She must have known she was ill with typhoid and TB; she was coughing a lot and knew she would not make it. So she would give us her food and eat practically nothing herself.'

Indeed, food had become so scarce by the end of the war, coming in small rations of thin gruel, black pieces of bread, or if they were lucky a piece of white bread, that families often fought among themselves over the meagre portions. Suzi's mother and brother at one point had to fight with another mother and son in the same hut in order to hold on to the extra portion that was meant for her. The incident severely weakened their mother and later she became so ill that she was moved away to a different hut. 'I remember her getting sick and I wasn't allowed to see her, even though my brother was. I was very annoyed about that. I also wondered why she didn't come back to us. You don't know what death is at that age; you just know that you don't see the person anymore and you don't know why. I thought she'd abandoned us.'

Small incidents still come back to Suzi of how they managed to survive through these days with their mother already dying. She eventually died of TB shortly after liberation. Suzi was perhaps too young to be frightened by the general sense of doom which hung over the camp at the latter end of the war when she and her family arrived there, but she recalls the early memory of being taught not to speak to any of the Nazi camp guards.

'I remember coming face to face with a Nazi and standing there petrified. He was smoking. I was told never to say a word and I didn't know what to do. He beckoned me to come over. So I went over, because you don't really have much of a choice. He put his hand in his pocket and I noticed then that he was eating something. He offered some to me and I can tell you that anything, any extra food, was a huge bonus. So after he gave me this piece of food, he told me to run off. I went away and gave some to my brother, but whoever was looking after us came out and gave me such a telling off. I couldn't understand why. Here I was with some extra food and then I'm being told off. They were afraid that by wandering off like that, something would happen to me.'

For many years, as Suzi was growing up in Ireland, she had a recurring dream of torture, which turns out to have been subconsciously linked to her time in the camp. But since she had been so young at the time of liberation, the dreams could only be dismissed, even in her own mind, as fabrications. It was recently while watching a television documentary on the children of victims meeting the children of perpetrators, that the dream could be connected with the stark reality of Belsen.

'I was watching a programme on TV, and one man was telling of an incident where they tortured people in the camp. The man was crying as he was telling this story. As I heard it, I felt as if I would pass out, because I remembered it myself. It was the nightmare I used to have as a child. You don't go around telling people your dreams, you just think – that was a nightmare. There was a big log fire and what looked to me like a big frying pan, but was some kind of a cast iron pot on the top of the fire. A man was brought out naked and was made to sit on the pot on the fire and you could smell his flesh as they were burning him. I don't know whether they put some oil or fat in.

'When I heard this man on TV speak about this, I remembered everything from my own dream. The man would have eventually died this way, burning in a huge frying pan. It is when this man recounted how everybody in the camp was forced to stand and witness what was taking place, that I could remember myself and my mother and my brother standing in front of this scene.

'I remember my mother trying to shield our eyes, trying to turn us away from what was going on. And one of the guards came over and hit her. He said they must see, they must see. We didn't want her to be hit again, so we turned and looked at this. And I had completely forgotten about it until I started having these nightmares. So it wasn't a nightmare, but just something I would be subconsciously remembering. It was quite startling to realise that it was reality, not a dream – something we had actually witnessed.'

Suzi Diamond feels that having gone through these traumatic experiences early in her life is what makes her memory so accurate now. 'I don't think of it every day, but it's always with me. With my memories, there is a bit here and a bit there. It's not like a whole episode or a whole day. It's just incidents.

'We lost everything. We lost our home, our nationality, our language, our parents. It's like being in a wilderness. It has a great impact when you are a child, because you've got nothing to hold on to except these memories.'

Around the day of liberation, there was a great deal of confusion. Suzi did not realise what freedom meant, only that the camp was filled with noise and shouting. Everyone was very happy, she didn't know why. 'Suddenly we didn't have to be afraid of soldiers in uniform any more.' Initially Suzi was very ill with typhus and there were fears for her life. She remembers her brother Terry standing by her cot all the time as she recovered. Another memory that returns now is the first taste of chocolate, when she saw two soldiers eating this strange black stuff.

'Horrible, I thought, but they said it was good and gave me some. I tasted it and it was nice and I ran back to Terry to give him half. I never forget the taste and I've been addicted to chocolate ever since.'

One of her strongest memories was that of Zoltan Zinn, one of the other orphans of Belsen, lying ill in a bed next to hers. She remembers Zoltan as they lay out on deck on the ferry to Malmö in Sweden where they were sent to recuperate before being brought to Ireland.

'I was always with Zoltan or beside him. I remember being on the plane to Ireland, again beside Zoltan. The plane ride was bumpy and everyone was getting sick. I got sick all over my dress. I remember Zoltan looking very pale and I thought he was going to die. I think you can see from the picture that when we arrived off the plane in Dublin, we were pretty washed out and exhausted.' On arrival, the children spent some time recovering together at Fairy Hill Hospital in Howth, before being adopted by their respective families.

Fifty years later, Suzi looks back over the sheer chance which brought her to her Irish sanctuary away from her past, almost as though she has now discovered her past for the first time. It seemed important for the orphans of Belsen to try and forget what had happened in Europe and to live their own lives; as such, the children who came to Ireland were never encouraged to talk about the Holocaust, to dwell on their family tragedies or to seek out their home towns and relatives. They were given new homes, new parents, new lives. They had everything a child can expect from a normal environment.

The books written by Dr Robert Collis and Han Collis were not prominent on the bookshelves of their home. Like most of Irish society in the 1950s, the attitude tended towards the containment of feelings and emotional issues. Unlike today, it was generally considered undignified and damaging to discuss anything personal or emotionally problematic, and perhaps, in the case of these orphans from Belsen, their past was too potentially destructive. The respected view of Dr Collis at the time was to shelter these traumatised and impressionable children from being exposed to the horror of what they had just come through. Suzi Diamond never remembers talking to her brother about Belsen. And except for one brief meeting as a child, when Suzi went for a visit to the Collis's home in Fitzwilliam Square, she and Zoltan never saw each other again until they met in the Royal Marine Hotel in Dun Laoghaire in June 1994.

'Nowadays, if you have a trauma in your life, you are encouraged to talk it out. People go through therapy to get things out of their system. In those days, the idea was that you would keep it to yourself. We were separated from anyone who had anything to do with the past. So we were afraid to talk about it. And because you suppressed it in childhood, it makes it all harder to talk about in later life.'

For Suzi and Zoltan, their emotional meeting was taken up by their childhood recollections and how, in spite of warm memories of their upbringing in Ireland, the Belsen tragedy has affected them deeply underneath. It was Suzi's impression that they seemed to have belonged to the same family and were now reunited after years of absence. 'Even after all this time, it wasn't like meeting a stranger. I immediately felt the same way as then, that I wanted to protect him. Even though he was older than I was, he was often much more ill and I used to help feed him. I regard him as a brother and the years between have just slipped away.'

Now in their fifties, with grown up children of their own, and half a century gone by, both Suzi and Zoltan feel that it is the right time to make sense of their past and the recollections which have remained concealed for so long. It was extraordinary how they were both in agreement so often about the similar ways in which the Holocaust had irrevocably affected their personalities. Like Zoltan, Suzi still wonders if she might have been a different person.

'It has made me distrusting. It takes a long, long time before I can form a proper relationship with people. We were taught to fear people, except for those in our own little circle. I'm claustrophobic. I'm obsessed with cleanliness. I get panicky if I'm going somewhere I haven't been before. I trust only what is familiar.'

6

Ettie Steinberg

There was one known Irish woman who lost her life in the death camps of Nazi Germany. Her name was Esther (Ettie) Steinberg, and every year in September her brother Jack Steinberg, who lives in Terenure, Dublin, holds a day of commemoration for her. Like the remaining members of the family, Rosie and Bessie now in London, Fanny in Toronto, and Solly in Jerusalem, he lights a 'Yortzeit' candle for twenty-four hours to remember Ettie. They attend a service at a local synagogue to recall how Ettie, her Belgian husband Vogtjeck and their two-year-old son, Leon, were caught in a Nazi 'action' in Toulouse, sent to Drancy outside Paris, and then on to Auschwitz where they were instantly put to death in the gas chambers on 4 September 1942. The details came to light, years later, from the meticulous Nazi records of the transportation and execution of Jews in the death camps.

In 1924, the Steinberg family originally left Mukachevo in Czechoslovakia and went to London with their seven children. In general, the Jews in Europe were said to be a mobile race and thought nothing of setting up home in a new country. Aaron Steinberg worked in the salt business and in 1928, when Jack Steinberg was ten years old and Esther was fourteen, they moved to

Ireland and settled at 28 Raymond Terrace, South Circular Road in Dublin. Esther went to private classes to learn English and also took up dressmaking, working for Henrietta's dress shop on Henry Street.

Jack Steinberg's wife remembers her well from that time. 'She was a beautiful girl, tall and slim with wonderful hands. She was a fantastic dressmaker and embroiderer.'

In July 1937, Ettie Steinberg married Vogtjeck Gluck, a Belgian goldsmith with a thriving business in Antwerp. The Gluck family had also come from the town of Mukachevo but had gone to live in Belgium from where they kept in touch with the Steinberg family. Vogtjeck came over to Dublin to visit the Steinbergs where it was hoped that a match would be made between himself and Ettie. They immediately liked each other and some time later a date was set for the wedding. Jack Steinberg recalls the mood in the family at the time of the announcement.

'Of course we knew that if she married Vogtjeck she would be leaving to live in Belgium. We were all sorry to see her go, but we knew that she would have a comfortable life. And we would all be visiting each other.'

Vogtjeck was twenty-four and Ettie was twenty-two when the wedding took place in Dublin on 22 July 1937 and the couple went to live in Antwerp. Of the people in the wedding photograph, both Vogtjeck's mother and five-year-old niece, who had travelled over from Belgium, were also to die at the hands of the Nazis.

Letters arrived home regularly from Ettie and some time later they had a baby boy named Leon. But then the war broke out in 1939 and the family at home in Ireland became increasingly worried for their safety. When the German army inevitably turned westwards to take Holland, Belgium and France, Ettie, Vogtjeck and their son were forced to flee Belgium.

In 1940/41, along with many Jewish refugees who had already fled Germany and other occupied countries in the east for Belgium, the young Gluck family moved on to temporary safety in France. They spent almost two years on the run, eventually ending up staying in a hotel in Toulouse where they thought they would be less conspicuous. When they left Belgium, they had no way of bringing any of their wealth with them and Vogtjeck made solid gold buttons, which Ettie covered with cloth and sewed onto her coat.

But late in 1942, the Nazi terror caught up with them in the hotel in Toulouse. With the sanction of the Vichy government in France which collaborated with the Nazis throughout the war, the roundup of Jews included the cities and towns in the south. Despite the strong protests and in particular the strong condemnation of the Nazis by the Catholic Archbishop of Toulouse, the Jews were taken from their homes and businesses and were brought to internment camps throughout France. The Nazis ordered the arrest of all Catholic priests who sheltered Jews. Relatives were initially told they could visit internees, only to find themselves included in their numbers and deported. There were eleven deportations in August 1942 from camps in the south of France to concentration camps in Germany and Poland; one of them from nearby Lyons contained 4,000 unaccompanied children. The Gluck family had undoubtedly become part of these particular transports and were taken first to Drancy, north of Paris, before being sent to Auschwitz.

Until September 1940, the Steinberg family continued to receive letters from Ettie and Chaskel (Vogtjeck's Hebrew name). The letters were normally stamped and passed by the Irish and German censors. The Steinbergs were increasingly worried that something would happen to Ettie and her family. Because of the censors, they wrote their letters in a coded jollity which made everything seem fine on the surface. Reading between the lines, the letters from the family expressed their fears about the war and hoped for their safety, in particular Ettie's two-year-old son Leon of whom they had heard so much.

It was only when a letter sent by her brother Solly, who was studying in Trinity College at the time, was returned with the remark *parti sans laisser d'adresse* (departed without leaving a forwarding address), that the family began to fear the worst. The envelope bears the seal *Geoeffnet* and *An Scrudoir d'Oscail* of both German and Irish authorities.

My Dear Ettie and all,

Last week we received two letters from you; written on the 9th and 29th Sept (1940). To-day we received a letter from Chaskel [Vogtjeck] from the 3rd August. Chaskel's letter was very heart-rending, but I hope that now he is together with you, and you are all all right.

Last week I managed to persuade the Red Cross here and they allowed us to send you a parcel of clothes. The society opened and censored the parcel here, and they sent it to Switzerland, and from there they sent it to you. I hope by the time you'll get this letter you will already have received the parcel. I wanted to send many more things but the parcel was too heavy, so they sent some things back.

It is so pleasant to read your descriptions of baby. We would all love to see him walk about and talk already. It must be quite confusing for him now as to what language to speak.

I am sure you are interested in some news from here, but it is not advisable to write too much, and that's why I always write post-cards. Ma and Da are keeping well T.G. Louis and his family are well too. The kids are running about as may be expected and are as sensible as old men.

Fanny and her husband are too living a quiet and peaceful life. About ourselves we are just carrying on normally. I myself go to Trinity, but am very worried about you and that interferes with my studying.

Every day, people ask about you, and there remains for me to say nothing but to wish you well, and to look after yourself, Chaskel and darling baby and keep as well as possible, and to wait and hope to God for better times which are bound to come, when we shall see each other again and relate to us all your experience.

Your dear brother, Solly

By 1942, the Steinberg family in Dublin had managed to obtain visas through the Home Office in Belfast for Ettie and her family to travel to Northern Ireland. The visas were sent straight on.to Toulouse, but again the envelope was returned, having arrived one day after the Gluck family's arrest and deportation.

At the Yad Vashem (Holocaust Museum) in Jerusalem, only five years ago, Solly Steinberg eventually discovered the true details of what happened to Ettie and her young family. Jack Steinberg and other members of the family had tried to trace them for years through the Red Cross, even writing to the Vatican and other sources to get information. 'We took it for granted that something must have happened to them, although we hoped against hope that it had not. The particular transport that they were on was sent immediately to the gas-chambers on arrival in Auschwitz. So the three of them went straight to their death. They weren't given a chance, nothing. This is all recorded in Yad Vashem in Jerusalem. Everything is written down, every name, every transport and the time it arrived,' says Jack.

The information that Solly Steinberg found in Jerusalem is taken from the precise record of all the deportations from Drancy to Auschwitz. The train journey would have followed the route Bourget-Drancy, Compiègne, Laon, Reims, Neuberg (frontier), Auschwitz. In the heat of September, the inhuman conditions began when deportees were packed into cattle trucks on the night before departure. The overcrowded train would have spent a full night on the tracks of Bourget-Drancy station, ready for the punctual 8:55 a.m. departure. There was one bucket for sanitary needs, but this soon overflowed and people would have been forced to relieve themselves on the floor. With stops along the way, usually with the occupants remaining inside where they had hardly enough space to sit, the journey to Auschwitz, with little or no water, took two to three days.

The Nazi records show that Vogtjeck Gluck, Esther Gluck and Leon Gluck departed from Gare du Bourget-Drancy at 8:55 a.m. on 2 September 1942 and arrived in Auschwitz on 4 September. On arrival at Auschwitz, people were normally separated and had their belongings taken from them. Some people were selected for work and had their heads shaved. Many would have been ordered to remove their clothes and were brought straight into what they were lead to believe were delousing chambers. Because their names are recorded together, Jack Steinberg believes that Ettie and her family would not have been separated, and that they would have gone directly to their death together.

'My father had five brothers. Three were lost, two from Czechoslovakia, and one from France. Another brother was living in Israel at the time and he survived. Two of his brothers lost their wives and families, large families with seven or eight children each. Their brother who lived in France was taken to Belsen, but his wife survived by hiding in a farmhouse in France right throughout the war. My cousin in London was only a child of eleven when she saw her own father lined up in Auschwitz. She ran over to him and he didn't recognise her with her hair shaved off, but she recognised him. But then he told her to run away from him. She lost all her brothers and sisters. I would say that, all in all, in excess of fifty members of my family died in the Holocaust. My grandparents both died too. There was just no trace of them.'

There was one more correspondence from Ettie Steinberg before she disappeared. The family received a card which was written by her on the journey to Auschwitz. The card, which has since gone missing during a break-in at the Steinberg's office in Dublin where it was kept in a safe, bore the last message in Ettie's handwriting. The heartbreaking words were never shown to their mother. 'We decided not to show it to our mother since she was always grieving about Ettie. In fact, we never told her anything about her death. My father and mother never spoke about it. It died with them.

'It really was a miracle that we got this postcard. It was thrown out of the train by Ettie on the way to Poland. Somebody must have picked it up and posted it. It passed the German censor and the Irish censor too. Both stamps were on it. And it was written in code. She wrote: "Uncle Lechem, we did not find, but we found Uncle Tisha

B'av." The translation of the Hebrew word 'Lechem' is bread and 'Tisha B'av' is the Jewish fast day commemorating the destruction of the temple. Her message meant that they had no food and were on their way to their death.'

7

Sabina Shorts

'There will come a time when the living will envy the dead.' Sabina (Wizniak) Shorts still remembers her mother uttering these ominous words in the Warsaw ghetto. That was shortly before Sabina left for Ireland. A fictitious letter from her father helped Sabina to make it to safety in Ireland where she still lives in the Dublin suburb of Rathfarnham. Through an extraordinary set of circumstances, she managed to join her father, who had come to Ireland ahead of her. Her sister Gina escaped to Israel, though, tragically, Sabina was forced to leave her mother and her younger sister Asta behind to the fate of Nazis.

Along with many other Berlin Jews, Sabina's family had lost their home and their possessions when they were forced to leave the German capital and go to the Warsaw ghetto before the war started. 'We lived in a side street, just five minutes away from the *Kurfürstendamm* in Berlin. Today it's called millionaire's row. It was a beautiful area with wonderful restaurants and cafés outside. My parents often used to go out in the evening and sit in these cafés. You would see all the film stars there, like Marlene Dietrich and many others. There were no airs or graces about anyone. A friend and I used to go around collecting their autographs.

'There was always music playing. Berlin was so full of life, it was incredible. It was inspiring to me, and when I was fourteen years of age, I made up my mind to be a singer. But I could never realise this ambition, and this has always been very painful to me.'

Life had become difficult for Jews in Berlin. Her father was a diamond merchant and was lucky to be in a position to bring some diamonds with him when he left. The Jewish community became more and more isolated, with Jewish merchants boycotted and their children shunned by classmates. For Sabina's family, everything came to a head one evening and she will never forget the circumstances in which they had to leave Berlin behind.

'My mother, my sister and I went out to buy some shoes in Berlin. We were a bit delayed and when we came home it was already dark. A neighbour stood outside the door and she said: "I have to tell you, there was a black car full of SS men in leather coats, and they were asking for you." When my mother heard that, she said we immediately had to go into the house and pack up our belongings, warm clothes etc., and to leave behind anything we could not carry.

'My younger sister Asta was ten years of age at the time. She kept asking why we had to go away. But my mother remained very quiet and calm. She said: "Just do as I tell you." And I remember as I was packing my clothes, thinking about my grandparents who had had to leave Russia because of pogroms, and thinking about the persecution of Jews in the Spanish Inquisition, and about my father, who actually escaped from Warsaw because they wanted to take him into the army, where life for a Jew would have been impossible.

'Here was I, in the twentieth century, having to leave the country that I loved. Nothing had changed. At this moment I felt deeply and emotionally hurt that this could happen to us. I was sixteen, and when you're that age you have dreams about the future and what you want to do. I no longer had any say in the matter. In one hour, we packed everything. We looked like refugees. We hardly had enough cases. My younger sister asked my mother if she should take her school books with her, and my mother said: "No, leave them."

'When the taxi took us to the station, I looked back and said, one day I'll come back again. We sat in the train on the way to Warsaw and were quiet. Not a word was said. My mother was very sad. In the Warsaw ghetto, it was strange that nobody ever laughed. Even the children didn't laugh. The housing was terrible. With such big families, it was extremely overcrowded and life was very hard.'

Even before the rumours of mass killings had reached the ghetto of Warsaw, heightening the fear among Jewish inhabitants, there were queues of people seeking visas to escape the inevitable terror. But the German borders were sealed, and without a visa, the notion of sanctuary in other countries like Ireland had become virtually impossible.

Sabina's family was plunged into the squalor and collective sense of doom of the Warsaw ghetto. Her mother's words echo the resignation and descending helplessness which pervaded the ghetto at the time. Under German occupation, Warsaw is remembered for the conditions of absolute terror which existed when Jews were locked inside the walls of the ghetto, not knowing when the time would come for them, or their loved ones, to be taken away. Indeed, even before they were transported to the death camps, the clearing of the ghettos alone would bring a level of brutality and spontaneous murder to the streets of Warsaw that would match any of the camps. The Warsaw ghetto uprising became the scene of one of the few acts of resistance to the Nazis and resulted in the most severe reprisals.

Through an extraordinary twist of fate, however, Sabina's father had managed to get himself to Ireland and sent a fabricated letter which helped her to escape the ghetto and follow him. The queues outside the offices of the British Embassy were already so long that there was no point in joining them. What Sabina did then was to phone up to plead her special case, following the fabricated line that an aunt in Ireland was very ill. Eventually she managed to speak to an official who was sufficiently moved by her invented story to grant her a exit visa. Once Sabina was in Ireland, the plan then was to try and work on some way of getting her mother and sister out too. But they were less fortunate and, at the age of fifteen, Asta was taken away to Majdeneck concentration camp where she died. Their mother, Dora, was among the thousands who met their death in the Warsaw ghetto.

Of all the Jews who came under the dictatorship of the Third Reich, the Berlin Jews were perhaps the most integrated, taking part in all aspects of German economic and cultural life of the city. Unlike the Polish Jews, of whom only around 10 per cent were said to be integrated with the general community, the German Jews had been encouraged to come to Berlin and take part. By the time the Nazis came to power, the Jews in the capital formed an integral part of all business and social life there; in fact, leading the way in many of the arts and sciences. And the huge number of cross marriages in Berlin forced the Nazis to back down and pardon the Jewish husbands of 5,000 Berlin women, who went on a spontaneous protest march at their removal from society.

The history of Berlin and its Jews is perhaps the best example of how violence in the streets led to the swift rise of Nazi omnipotence in Germany and the ultimate destruction of Jewry in Europe. Even under Bismarck, Germans in Berlin had a legendary respect for uniform, and ordinary people in the streets would step off the pavement to allow a soldier or a police officer to pass. In the 30s the new Nazi party sought to exploit this reverence or intrinsic German fear of uniform, and to make obedience a virtue in its own right. Under Joseph Goebbels, the city soon became *Judenfrei* or free of Jews according to the 'final solution'. Of the estimated 160,000 Jews in Berlin at the beginning of the war, only 6,100 were to survive.

In the early years of the war, news had reached the inhabitants in Berlin of horrific mass executions of Jews in Poland and Russia. Many eyewitness accounts exist, often of Jews who had been forced to become gravediggers for their own people, bore testimony to brutal murders and mass graves seething with the moaning victims who were buried half dead in pits. The spread of these alarming rumours prompted Nazi *Gauleiters* (Governors) such as Hans Frank to call for the introduction of more clinical measures against the Jews.

L a n d	Zahl
A. Altreich	131.800
Ostmark	43.700
Ostgebiete	420.000
Generalgouvernement	2.284.000
Bialystok	400.000
Protektorat Böhmen und Mähren	74.200
Estland – judenfrei –	
Lettland	3.500
Litauen	34.000
Belgien	43.000
Dänemark	5.600
Frankreich / Besetztes Gebiet	165.000
Unbesetztes Gebiet	700.000
Griechenland	69.600
Niederlande	160.800
Norwegen	1.300
B. Bulgarien	48.000
England	330.000
Finnland	2.300
Irland	4.000
Italien einschl. Sardinien	58.000
Albanien	200
Kroatien	40.000
Portugal	3.000
Rumänien einschl. Bessarabien	342.000
Schweden	8.000
Schweiz	18.000
Serbien	10.000
Slowakei	88.000
Spanien	6.000
Türkei (europ. Teil)	55.500
Ungarn	742.800
UdSSR	5.000.000
Ukraine 2.994.684	
Weißrußland aus-	
schl. Bialystok 446.484	
Zusammen: über	11.000.000

The 1944 Wannsee Conference document outlining the Jewish population throughout Europe, including 4,000 in Ireland.

(Above) Edith, Zoltan and Aladar in Slovakia before their deportation.
(Below) Zoltan and Edith in Belsen after liberation in June 1945.

Bloodstained barbed wire along with Nazi insignia from Belsen concentration camp.
(Courtesy of the Jewish Museum, Dublin)

The Belsen children arriving in Dublin Airport, 1947 (From the left): Terry, Edith, Suzi (on Dr Robert Collis's shoulder), Evelyn and Zoltan (carried by Irish air hostess).

The Belsen children at Fairy Hill Hospital, Howth (Zoltan in bed).

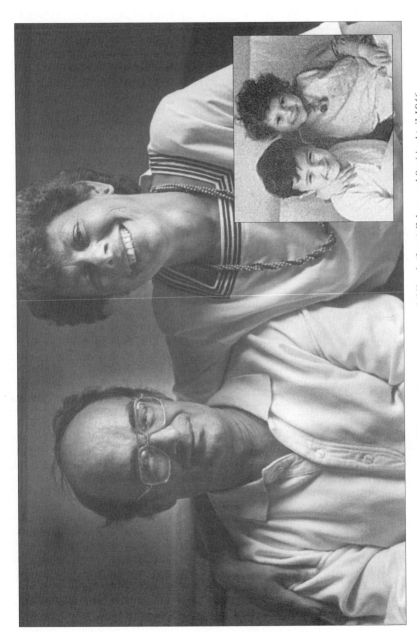

Zoltan and Suzi in June 1994, their first meeting since childhood. (Inset) Zoltan and Suzi in April 1946.

'The thing that moved me more than anything else was this huge pile of shoes... tiny little children's shoes, and high-heeled shoes, and half-broken old men's shoes.'

Dr Han Collis at home in County Wicklow.

Wedding photograph of Ettie Steinberg (the only known Irish victim of the Holocaust. She died in Auschwitz). Behind her (right), her Belgian husband Vogtjeck Gluck and her brothers Jack and Solly (far right). Beside her (right) is Vogtjeck's mother, who also died, along with Vogtjeck's five-year-old niece on the ground (centre).

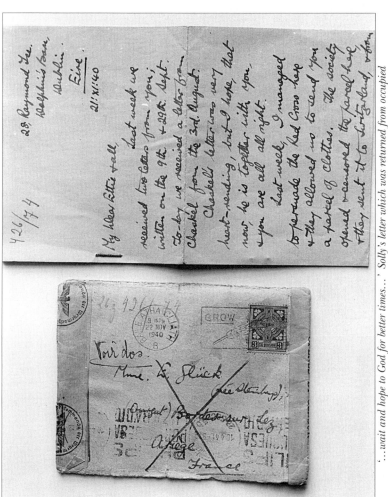

426/74

28, Raymond Lee,
Rathmines Town,
Dublin.
Eire.
21. XI. '40

My dear Ettie + all,
        last week we
received two letters from you,
written on the 9th. + 29th. Sept.
To-day we received a letter from
Chankel from the 3rd. August.
Chankel's letter was very
heart-rending, but I hope, that
now, he is together with you,
you are all all right.
        last week, I managed
to persuade the Red Cross here
+ they allowed us to send you
a parcel of clothes. The society
opened + censored the parcel here,
+ they sent it to Switzerland, from

'...wait and hope to God for better times...' Solly's letter which was returned from occupied
France bearing the remark – *'parti sans laisser d'adresse'*.
(Courtesy of the Jewish Museum, Dublin)

Agnes Bernelle with her parents. During the 'Golden 20s', her father owned four theatres before he left Berlin, arriving in London with only a gold cigarette case.

Doris Segal as a baby.

Doris with her parents in the Sudetenland.

Doris's grandparents, who died in Auschwitz in 1943.

Rosel Siev's parents, Martin and Karoline Wolff. These are the passport photos which her sister Hanna (saved by Oskar Schindler) carried with her through the camps.

Rosel in Dublin 1994.

Rosel aged sixteen.

'The Nazis subjected me to a life of passive torture that will stay with me until the end of my days.'

Helen as a six-year-old.

Dance saved her life.

Helen Lewis at home in Belfast.

(Copyright: Pacemaker)

Geoffrey Phillips (top right) and the only two remaining photographs; (top) with his parents (right) and uncle; (below) at his Jewish school in Wanne-Eickel (far right in front of teacher) shortly before he left home on the Kindertransport.

Yellow star which had to be worn by all Jews over the age of six.
(Courtesy of the Jewish Museum, Dublin)

From Ireland in 1940, Sabina Shorts wrote to Hans Frank, the *Gauleiter* of Poland, to find out about her mother and sister, as well as her grandparents. 'I was neutral here, and my name was not a Jewish name. So when I was here in neutral Ireland, somebody suggested that I should write to Hans Frank and ask how my mother and sister, and grandparents were in Warsaw. I got a letter back from him saying that my mother and sister were fine, but because my grandparents were getting older, they were a little bit frail. So this news made me feel better.

'But, in fact, it was a very clever and sinister act. To tell me that everything is wonderful. Because he realised that Ireland was neutral, he knew that such a letter would make a very good impression here. I didn't think of it at the time. I was taken in. It was only later on when I spoke to my father, that I opened my eyes. "Do you know," he said, "this is a wonderful advertisement for them."

'My mother was murdered in the Warsaw ghetto. It is far too dreadful for me to talk about it, or even to think about. And you can imagine how awful it must have been for her when they came and took Asta away. Neither of them knew where she was going. I cannot bear to think about it.'

By 1941/42, each new directive from Berlin was intended to make the action against Jews less conspicuous, and the Jews were increasingly brought to the their place of death by an elaborate series of lies and deception. The killing operations began to take on a more discreet and sinister nature, with specially designed, airtight execution trucks in which the exhaust was turned in on the occupants. But even the disposal of thousands of corpses remained a problem and finally, the refinement of the extermination included the construction of gas-chambers and incinerators. Such was the level of deception that Jewish victims were often spoken to in polite tones and given many promises of being reunited with their relatives. There are reports of Jews letting out a cheer on arrival at Auschwitz when they were told that they had been destined for work. Other reports tell of Jews arriving at death camps dismissing what they believed were cruel jokes, when told by other inmates that the smell and smoke coming from the chimneys was that of incinerated comrades.

Three and a half years after Sabina Shorts had arrived in the Warsaw ghetto, she got a vital four-week visa to visit Ireland. At twenty years of age, with very little money, she stayed for four weeks with a Dublin family. As the visa came to an end, Sabina received a visit from an official in the External Affairs Department, who informed her that she had to leave Ireland. Acting as a deportation officer, the official reminded her that her visa was up. 'I didn't plead with him. I was just resigned to what would happen.'

The alien office decreed that she should be sent to Belfast. At the train station, the deportation officer met her on a given date to make sure that Sabina Wizniak left the jurisdiction. 'I must have looked a pitiful sight with all my suitcases. I didn't plead with him or ask him anything. He voluntarily suggested an alternative.'

Visualising the horrific world she would have to return to, the official took pity on her and suggested that she only needed to take two stops on the train, and then come back again. He would say nothing. But then he relented even further and told her not to get on the train at all, just to go home. He would let on he had seen her departing the country.

To Sabina Shorts, having come from the rigid enforcement of anti-Jewish measures, this relaxed attitude towards the law seemed like an enormous blessing. She could hardly believe it. But it was merely the beginning of a series of fortunate encounters with benign Irish officialdom, ready to turn a blind eye to her presence in Dublin. The futility of applying for another visa, and the lingering threat of expulsion, meant that Sabina would have to find a new place to stay. When the widow she had stayed with needed her room for her daughter who was returning home, she saw an advertisement in the *Evening Mail* for a room to let.

'I went around to the house in South Circular Road. A young girl answered the door. She was very polite and invited me into the drawing room to sit down. It was a homely house, and I noticed a piano in the corner. When the owner, James Stapleton, came into the room, he had a fiddle and bow in his hands which he had been playing. I immediately saw that he was a warm and kindly man. At that time, I was afraid of talking to anyone, and I must have had a very shy expression on my face. But he immediately made me feel at home. He showed me my room and said that I was very welcome to take it. I think I paid around 10 shillings per week at that time.'

Having to leave her present accommodation immediately, she wanted to know how soon she could move in. Mr Stapleton instantly said: 'Go and get your bags and you can move in this afternoon.'

'So that's what I did. I went and got my case and moved into the room. It was a lovely bright room, and then little Jimmy came upstairs and said: "Would you please come down and have a cup of tea." To me this was really the limit. I went down and the table was laid with a beautiful apple tart. They kept saying: "You must eat." I had never met such kindness. And every night before bed they would say the rosary.

'I was very, very happy and secure in this house. His wife, Julia, was a lovely woman. I also got on very well with their two children, Jimmy and Vera; they were always mesmerised by my broken English. In fact I'm still in regular contact with them.

'But one day something awful happened. I saw Mr Stapleton coming down the stairs in a uniform and I realised that he was working for the Gardaí. I knew then that it would be impossible for me to stay in the house any longer. What if he lost his job because of me, I thought. Things could become difficult for me also. I asked if I could speak to him, and that evening I told him that I had to go, though I could not tell him why.'

When Sabina sat in the drawing room that evening, explaining how she had to leave suddenly, James Stapleton was astonished and asked why. Did she not like the room any more? Was she not happy? He thought she liked living there and asked her if there was something wrong.

'"I love it here," I told him. "You've been like a family to me. And this is the first home I've had since I left Berlin. But I have to leave." I wanted to tell him the reason, but he stopped me. He put up his hand and he gave me a wink. He was smoking his pipe at the time and then he said: "You can only leave if you don't like it here. If you like it here, you're going to stay." And then I realised that he was very genuine and that he knew all about me.'

Once again, Sabina was overwhelmed at the kindness in the Stapleton home. She was given the breakfast room in the house which she used as a workshop for dressmaking. She bought a Singer sewing machine on hire purchase for half a crown a week and got down to earning a livelihood. And when things became difficult for her financially, the Stapletons would waive the rent. Sabina soon became part of the family and she remembers the three and a half years she lived there as the happiest days of her life in Ireland.

In May 1941, when the German Luftwaffe flew off target and dropped bombs in Dublin, Sabina recalls being woken up from her sleep. She spent the night praying. Afterwards, she was able to discuss everything more openly with James Stapleton. 'He asked me if I was worried. He said the "Gerries" would never be allowed to invade Ireland. He said Ireland had put up with one invasion, they would bottle up the whole lot of them. In any case, there was a big shed out in the back which nobody knew about and he would hide me in it.

'In Ireland I found peace. In this household, where everybody was so good to me, I became very close to all of them, particularly the children. For the first time in many years I found some sort of security and warmth in my life. Of course, on many occasions I would become disheartened, not knowing what had become of my mother and younger sister in Warsaw. But the Stapleton family knew of my troubles and were always very supportive and good to me in those times. They wouldn't let me be on my own upstairs. They would hate to see me sad and often called me downstairs for a meal.

'He restored my faith in Christians. In Berlin it was all rejection. As a child, so many of my Christian friends were not allowed to play with me any more. Their parents would send me away from their houses. In Europe, everything was so depressing. And here in Ireland, everybody took things so easy. People would laugh and have a drink.

'Later on, Mr Stapleton would also talk to me about Germany and about my mother and sister. He told me not to worry and that I should build up my own life here. '

Because of her illegal status in Ireland, however, Sabina, who is now writing her life story, was unable to meet openly or regularly with her father. In 1945, he left for London and then on to Israel where he spent the rest of his life in the company of his daughter Gina, grieving for his wife and youngest daughter whom he was unable to save. Later, Sabina married a London furrier named Monty Shorts and they had two children. But long before she got married, she spent years hoping to put things right on an official level and eventually applied for a full immigrant status in Ireland.

'The judge was a very nice man. He told me to come up and sit beside him so that I could tell him what had happened to me and my family. He even congratulated me on my English and said he would hope to speak German as well. I felt terrible. I was a young girl and everyone was looking at me. He said that he would grant me a residence permit, but that he would have to fine me the minimum penalty of five pounds because I had been in the country illegally. He also said that I would not be allowed to work.'

But once again the directive was not of the rigid Nazi type, but of a peculiar Irish nature which meant it was not to be taken literally. As long as nobody heard about it, the law was being upheld.

'I immediately paid my fine. I couldn't believe it was only five pounds. Then the strangest of all things happened. One of the officials from the Aliens Office came over to me and whispered: "Don't change anything. Just carry on the way you are." It was as much as telling me to keep on working. In fact, they told me much later that they all knew perfectly well that I was living and working here. But they never said a word.'

In 1987, Sabina Shorts was finally able to fulfil the promise she made to herself on the day she left Berlin in the taxi with her mother and sister and all their suitcases. For the first time, Sabina returned to the city of her youth to try and make sense of what had taken place there. She wanted to meet an old person, an old woman perhaps, who could tell her what it was like before and after Hitler.

'I saw an old woman sitting on a bench, and I sat down beside her. She was looking into space. She had a little dog beside her. A little savage-looking thing with ears sticking up in the air. He came over and barked and barked at me. I thought to myself, what's the matter with this dog, and without looking at me, the woman said: "You are sitting in my late husband's place, and Fritz doesn't like it."

'Then she told Fritz to sit down beside her and the dog obeyed. I turned to her and said: "I'm sorry that you lost your husband. But anyway, you must have a family to console you." She still never looked at me. But she said: "No. My three young boys were killed in the war."

'I remarked that every war claims its victims. So then she looked at me for the first time and said: "Why, did you lose anybody?" and I said: "Yes, my mother and my sister." Then she said: "They must have died that time when the bombs were dropped over Berlin." But I replied: "No, they were murdered by the Nazis."

'Well what can I tell you? Old and grey as she was, this woman got up from the bench and called her dog to follow her. "Come on, Fritz," she said. I looked at the bent figure of this old woman walking away, and only the little dog beside her to comfort her. All her family dead. I realised how war had sucked everyone in. But I had sympathised with her, and she didn't sympathise with me. That was very hurtful. Then I found myself looking into space like her, and I thought: is this what life is all about?'

8

Agnes Bernelle

*

With the rise of fascism in Germany during the 1930s, the thriving cultural life of Berlin suffered an immense blow as it fell into the grip of the Nazis. During the 'Golden Twenties', best remembered perhaps through legendary films such as *The Blue Angel* and *Cabaret*, Berlin played host to a great era of liberal innovation in the arts, particularly in film and on the stage. With its thirty-five theatres putting on everything from Max Reinhardt productions to revues and musicals, Berlin had become an integrated, indiscriminate adventure in which the Jews played a leading role. From this point of view alone, the Nazis spelled disaster. Even purely in cultural and artistic terms, removing the Jews ultimately represented an enormous loss to society.

Agnes Bernelle, the well-known Dublin actress, singer and writer, came from the Bernauer family, who played a prominent role in the artistic community of Berlin in the 20s and 30s. Her father, Rudolf Bernauer, who owned four of the theatres, was one of the most important stage directors in the city and also wrote plays and musicals. But even as early as 1928, the *Gauleiter* of Berlin, Joseph Goebbels, had condemned the city's cultural life as 'a melting pot of evil – prostitutes, drinking houses, cinemas, Marxism, Jews, strippers, negroes dancing, and all the vile offshoots of so-called 'modern art'.

The Nazis were quick to identify liberal arts as the greatest enemy of totalitarianism. Under their reign, all culture was swiftly sterilised and incorporated as an instrument of Nazi propaganda. Much of the artistic community, both Jewish and non-Jewish, fled.

For Agnes Bernelle, it was a singleminded ambition to become an actress that took her family out of Berlin in time, forcing them to send Agnes to school in London long before the transports began to the concentration camps. The fact that she had her heart set on acting, and knowing that the arts had become forbidden to Jews in Germany, convinced Agnes at the age of thirteen that she had to get out. In 1936, her father brought her to a boarding school in London.

'I was determined to go abroad. As a child I was very spoiled. I knew I wanted to be an actress, but I knew it would be impossible for me to act in Germany. I thought if I was going to have to act in another country, an accent wouldn't help my career. So I said to my father, "I don't care what country you go to, just leave and earn enough money to send me to boarding school somewhere, where I can learn the language.'

Anges Bernelle was born in Berlin in 1923. Her father, Rudolf Bernauer, was Jewish. Her mother, Emmy Erb, was Protestant. Anges was brought up as a Protestant until she was twelve or thirteen and then became Catholic. 'I remember going to school and seeing the ugly face of Hitler with his moustache on posters on those advertising columns on the street. I was in a Jewish school then, my first school, and little boys used to throw stones at his face and when I asked why, they told me that this was a nasty man who wanted to come and kill all the Jews. I started to worry about my father and for the first time I became aware that he was a Jew.

'I remember it almost more clearly than many other things. As you get older, your memory goes back further. I went to another school with about 500 girls. There were still some Jews there in 1930 and 1931, but they all gradually left. I hope they escaped and got away, I don't know. I was the only so-called 'non-Aryan' in the school. Obviously I must have been unhappy about it. I had to greet my teachers with "Heil Hitler" every morning and I hated all that. I think I became Catholic out of protest.

'They took away the parson who had been teaching us religion and they gave his classes to a singing teacher, who was a terrible Nazi. All he ever did was to rail against the freemasons and the Catholics. We never got any instruction in religion. I made friends with the few Catholics in the school and this irritated the headmaster.'

Agnes Bernelle, who is writing her autobiography under the title *The Fun Palace*, remembers that there was no great panic while she still lived in Berlin. People just disappeared quietly. 'There was a lot of worry, concern, misery, sadness. The panic all started later on when they began to pick people up. Up until then if Jews could get a visa, they were let out, so it wasn't such a terminal thing.'

Her father became a Catholic, not just to conceal his Jewish status but out of a genuine preference for the Catholic faith. He had been educated by the monks in Budapest, where he had served as an altar boy when he was ten. The fact that his family was originally Hungarian seemed at first to grant them immunity from the Nazi decrees against the Jews. He had taken out German citizenship in order to run the theatres. But, ultimately, his Jewish ancestry would suffice to condemn him and his family under Nazi laws.

On the day Hitler came to power, Agnes's father and his partner fled Germany. They got as far as the border and were promptly arrested and put into jail. Agnes's mother went to look for her husband and eventually found him wandering around Munich where they had released him. At the age of eight, Agnes had been told none of this at the time. 'But children usually do find out what's going on. I remember other family members arriving at the house and they were all in tears and whispering.'

After her father's attempt to leave Germany, the authorities had confiscated his German passport. It meant that without papers, they would have to stay in Germany. Eventually, he was able to claim back his Hungarian citizenship.

'You had to go to Hungary once in twenty years to qualify for this. He thought he hadn't been back, but then my mother remembered a terrible row they had one night about how she wanted to go and see one of his plays performed in Budapest. Eventually they did go and that one night was enough to qualify for citizenship.'

In order to prove that he had been back to Budapest, however, her father needed to produce the confiscated passport bearing the Hungarian stamp. His passport was stored along with millions of other documents in the cellar of the Reichstag in Berlin.

'A friend of my father's was in the police force and he sent two policemen into the Reichstag cellar to search amongst the piles of confiscated papers. They found it and that's how we got our Hungarian passports. Otherwise we would never have been able to leave.'

By that time, however, Agnes's father thought less of the need to emigrate. Although his name had been taken off all playbills and his theatres sold off in forced auctions, he still received royalties on which the family could live. They were no longer well off, but they could exist. He was over forty and did not like the idea of moving to a new country and changing his working language. When Rudolf Bernauer finally left, he went first to Vienna and then to Paris. Fortunately, he did not decide to settle in either of these cities. It was only when Agnes herself had become so keen on acting and learning a new language that would allow her to pursue the profession, that he eventually agreed to bring her to London.

'He wasn't allowed to take anything with him. He went off with only a gold cigarette case. He pawned it in London. Within a year he had met some of his old friends from the film industry and he began writing scripts. He then got me over and sent me to boarding school.

'He couldn't bring my mother over to live at the time because he didn't have the money. Though she wasn't Jewish, she stayed in a Jewish boarding house in Berlin. She lived on the royalties and visited London occasionally, bringing over suits she had made for him in

Berlin. I went home for the holidays. We never asked ourselves why this Jewish boarding house was still allowed to operate in 1936.'

Among the occupants of the Jewish boarding house lived another non-Jewish German. 'I thought he was gorgeous; he always bought me sweets. One evening he invited my mother out to dinner. When she got there, she was confronted by two Nazi officials who said that they had been watching her. They said they knew that she was going to London all the time to visit her half-Jewish child and her Jewish husband.

'They said that she had betrayed her blood by marrying a Jew, but that they would give her a chance to redeem herself if she would do a bit of spying for them. My mother was absolutely terrified. She said she wasn't hungry, she wanted to leave the restaurant. There was a big black car outside and as they clicked their heels, one of the men pressed a huge wad of notes into her hand. She opened her hand and saw the bundle of notes starting to fly across the street.

'The men tried to pick up the money and this gave her a chance to get away. She ran like the wind back to the boarding house, got her passport and her fur coat, took a taxi to the station and sat all night in the waiting room, terrified that they would follow her. But they didn't think she would act so quickly. When she got to the frontier, she didn't know if her name was already there, but it wasn't. When she finally arrived in London, she was ill and terribly upset. Three weeks later war broke out. If this confrontation with the Nazis hadn't occurred, she would have been left behind in Berlin.

'We all got away. The person who unfortunately didn't get away was my aunt, my father's sister, Gisela. Her first husband died a natural death, so she was a widow when she fled to Amsterdam with her married daughter. But she was caught there by the Nazis and was taken to Belsen along with my cousin Ilma and her husband. My aunt remarried in Belsen concentration camp, though neither she nor her new husband survived.

'My cousin Ilma did survive. She spent five years in Belsen, though her husband died there. After liberation, at the age of forty, she went back to Amsterdam where she married the husband of a best friend who had died. She is well into her eighties now. She came to see us in London shortly after the war and gave us the whole horror story. I can't remember everything she told us but I think that my aunt and her husband died of malnutrition or dysentery. Ilma worked in the camp and this is what helped her to get through.'

Though Agnes did not suffer physically at the hands of the Nazis, she has been affected emotionally, and in recalling the story of her cousin, she falls silent, contemplating what might have become of her and her own parents had they stayed in Berlin.

After witnessing the horror at Belsen, her cousin was given the opportunity to go to another camp. 'At the end of the five years the SS came and offered them a chance to move. My cousin told me how at the time she thought she might as well get away from Belsen and all the awful memories of her family dying. So she volunteered and was put on a train. What she didn't know was that they were driving these trains into a lake. The Germans knew everyone else in the camp was dying, so they got the healthy ones onto the trains.

'The people in the camp had no idea how close the Americans and the British were, or how soon the war would be over. Ilma's train was the last one to leave. She was sitting in the carriage with hundreds of others when she heard shooting. The train stopped. Suddenly, white American helmets appeared, the Nazi guards jumped off the train and were shot, and the prisoners were still sitting on the train with no idea what was happening.

'After the war, in Amsterdam, Ilma met the husband of her deceased friend. He had been hidden in an attic by a Dutch woman for all those years during the war. Afterwards, they decided to get married and they set up home in Amsterdam. I visited them many years ago. Somehow, I imagined that anyone who had survived a concentration camp would be carrying that burden with them every day for the rest of their lives. But nature doesn't work that way. I couldn't believe it when I saw how she was worrying about mundane things like her knitting being finished or what tie her husband should wear out to dinner that night. It was all so terribly ordinary. It felt very strange. I was expecting them to behave like victims all the time.'

Agnes Bernelle has moved her entire life twice, once from Berlin to London and then from London to Dublin. It has affected her in that she feels that she does not belong to any nationhood or religion. 'I don't feel that I'm Jewish. I don't feel that I'm non-Jewish. I don't feel that I'm German, Hungarian or Irish. I don't feel that I'm English and yet I feel that I'm involved in all these things in a liberating way.'

She never wanted to return to Berlin. They offered her father one of his theatres back after the war in order to encourage the arts again in the city. 'But he couldn't go back. When you have gone through what he went through, you do not forgive easily. It took a long time before I could return to Berlin without that feeling of unease. I kept looking around at people and thinking who they were and what had they done during the war. It's only now that I'm old and most of those people are dead that I don't mind going. In fact I quite enjoy going back now. But it took many many years.

'I keep remembering how after my father left, I fell madly in love with a young man when I was just thirteen. He used to pursue my mother. He was in Nazi uniform. On *Kristallnacht*, he stood guard outside the Jewish shops while they were being smashed up. And when it was over he bought a large bunch of roses and expected to call on us to have tea with my mother. Of course, after what happened, my mother threw the roses in his face and told him never to come back. I remember being heartbroken about him. He was so handsome. Years later, a German school friend of mine met him when she was skiing. She said, "You're the man my friend Agnes was mad about when she was thirteen." So he obviously survived.'

Because Agnes Bernelle had been a part of Berlin under the Nazi years, she found herself unable to read about it or talk about it for a long time after the war. Somehow, she felt she could cope better with it in silence. 'I have always tried not to go and see films about the subject. In the end though I did make myself watch all these awful documentaries, and later, feature films such as *Sophie's Choice*. I thought I should watch it and I made my children watch.'

Looking back over history is not easy, she feels. Over the years Agnes has built up an ability to cut herself off, to protect herself from the graphic horror of the Holocaust. 'The only time I could not protect myself is when we visited Jerusalem, when I got to the Wailing Wall. I put my face into the wall and suddenly the whole thing hit me. All the protection just broke down and I started crying. I couldn't stop. That was the only time it got to me. Up until then I had known it was all appalling and awful but I didn't want to feel it until then, at the Wailing Wall in Jerusalem. I cried and cried, and couldn't stop for hours.'

9

Doris Segal

'I was about five years of age. I remember being disturbed in the middle of the night. My uncle came to the house and told my parents to pack up and get out immediately. When we left for Ireland, I remember saying goodbye to my grandparents and my mother saying to me: "Do you realise you may never see them again?"'

One night in 1937, Doris (Dorothea Klepper) Segal's parents fled their small Sudetenland town, got on the train and took their only child to Prague.

Doris left behind the swimming pool where she used to spend every day in the summer. She left behind the big three-storey house of her grandparents and the family-owned down-feather factory. Fortuitously, her father knew that a hat factory was being opened in Castlebar in the West of Ireland, and, posing as an expert in the manufacture of hats, managed to get a visa and move his family to safety out of Czechoslovakia. Doris never saw her grandparents again.

By the summer of 1938, although Hitler had not yet begun his aggression against the other nations of Europe, the Germans claimed the right to speak for and defend Germans everywhere. As a prelude to his plans for expansion, Hitler began to make claims in particular on the Sudeten Germans. This region of Czechoslovakia had never belonged to Germany, though when Austria had become subsumed into the Third Reich in March of that year, Hitler's pre-war posturing called for the annexation of this mainly German-speaking portion of Czechoslovakia which had formerly belonged to the Austro-Hungarian empire. After intense international debate, driven by Germany's threat of military force, other countries eventually bowed to Hitler's demands to annex the Sudetanland after the Munich conference of September 1938.

Like the 20,000 Jews of the Sudetenland, the Klepper family fled to safety and lived in Prague under the constant threat of further German expansion. By 1939, the 56,000 Jews in the capital were desperately seeking escape routes, to Poland and Hungary, to France and Holland, to Britain and Israel, Ireland and the USA if they could obtain visas. Hitler, who had been preparing the most advanced and highly trained army in the world, inevitably dispensed with the sham of diplomacy and by March 1939 marched into Czechoslovakia. Except for the few who managed to get exit visas, the Jews of the entire region became trapped.

Dorothea Klepper was born in 1932 in the small German-speaking town of Komotau in the Sudetenland. She was brought up in her grandparents' house in Kantstrasse where the ground floor was let; the grandparents lived on the first floor, and Doris lived with her parents on the second floor. At the back of the house, Doris remembers the sand pit she played in as a child.

'There was a beautiful park and lake in Komotau called the Allaunsee. They had different swimming pools with graduated areas for non-swimmers. I remember my cousin holding the straps of my bathing costume and teaching me to swim. In the winter we would ice-skate in the same lake that we swam in during the summer. I have very fond memories of that. I had a very happy childhood. I was born after nine years of marriage and had no brothers and sisters, so you can imagine how spoiled I was, especially by my grandparents.

'I called them Omi and Opa. Their names were Max and Klara Heller, and my grandfather and his brother owned a down-feather factory called 'Siegfried Heller und Bruder'. The factory is now derelict and sealed off. I believe my grandparents' house is in a terrible state. I have never been back, but my cousin, who lives in Israel, has sent me photos.'

Doris's father, Siegfried Klepper, worked as a *prokurist* or book-keeper in the 'Hugo Reiniger & Co' hat factory in Komotau. In order to get the visa to work in Ireland, he had to say that he was skilled in hat-making. After the long journey, the Klepper family arrived in Dublin where they waited for the Castlebar factory to be opened.

'I think it was summer 1938. I remember the long journey. Trains and boats. We came with a suitcase each and I had a little bag with my doll and a few other things. We lived in Monkstown initially, then in Sandymount, and later in one of the big houses on Pembroke Road. I often look back and think how difficult it must have been for my parents. Neither of them knew the language, although my mother had some knowledge of English from school.'

Doris's mother, Marguerite, had a hereditary hearing problem which was exacerbated by scarlet fever she had contracted just before Doris was born. She had to have a full-time nurse and Doris still remembers her last governess named Traute. She kept in touch with them later on after they had left Czechoslovakia and organised the delivery of many of their belongings to the West of Ireland.

'A gents' hat factory was being built in Castlebar by Senator John E. MacEllin with the assistance of an Austrian named Markus Witztum. A ladies' hat factory was being built at the same time in Galway. My father heard about these factories in Komotau. I never thought to ask my parents questions when they were alive, and now I'm sorry I haven't more details about my past.'

In Castlebar, Doris Segal went to the Convent of Mercy and learned everything through Irish. 'I loved it, especially writing in Irish with the old script. Even during the break, you had to speak in Irish, and it certainly didn't help me to learn other subjects. In fact it was quite useless. My Irish name was Doráis Ní Clipper. They would go "Klipper, Klapper, clip her in the ear."

'For my father it was difficult because he was originally from Poland. He found the pronunciation very hard and I used to help him with his English. Luckily my mother had learned English as a child and that helped her a lot, and although she was deaf, she was very good at lip-reading. But her accent was very strong. At home, though, we'd speak mostly in German, because it was easier for my mother to lip-read.'

The climate in the West of Ireland was another major factor for the family to contend with. The constant dampness, combined with the scarcity of coal during the war years, was hard for them to bear since they had come from a comparatively wealthy home in Sudetenland. 'We came from a comfortable background and to live in a damp, rented bungalow where we had to put turf into the range before you could cook on it, was all pretty new and difficult. I was a child and everything was an adventure and a challenge for me. But I didn't realise what my parents were going through.'

Apart from that, Doris Segal has happy memories of Castlebar, where her father was employed for twelve years in the hat factory until he developed a skin allergy from the sheep's wool which went into the making of the hats. He found it necessary to accustom himself to entirely new skills. He worked in the spinning department and had to learn about the operation of the machinery, which nearly cost him two of his fingers in separate accidents.

'In Castlebar everybody was very nice to me. In fact they were all fighting over me, the Protestants and the Catholics. So I went to church and I went to chapel too. It was all fun to me. When I was twelve, I went to the Hall School in Monkstown, County Dublin as a boarder. I thought I would love it, but they made me apple pie beds and used to tease me. At the same time I made very good friends and I'm still in touch with some of them.'

Doris Segal went on to train as a physiotherapist at Hume Street in Dublin, married and moved to Terenure. Her husband, Jack Segal, died seven years ago and their three children are all living abroad.

Doris's father, Siegfried, or Fred as he was known in Castlebar, was asked by the Local Defence Force, to teach physical training. Word had got out among his colleagues at the hat factory that he had a particular knowledge of gymnastics, which he had learned through the Sokol gymnastic organisation in the Sudetenland.

'He taught the local branch of the Local Defence Force how to perform drill and pyramids to the music of "The Merry Widow". They put on a fabulous exhibition with torches. The only stipulation was that he would have to give the commands in the Irish language which he managed by learning them off by heart. The ladies were also very interested in learning how to perform gymnastics, but unfortunately, they were forbidden from wearing trousers and shorts, so it was out of the question.'

All through the war years, Doris's parents kept a map of Europe on the wall of their Castlebar home. They would stick pins into it as they heard the ongoing news of the war. There was a constant atmosphere of waiting. They were anxious to hear of the fate of Doris's grandparents, left behind in Komotau, for whom it was impossible to get work permits in Ireland because they were too old.

'We got a couple of postcards from my grandparents during that time. We had no details at all of what happened to them. I know that my parents were trying to trace them for years through various offices and they even went to London to try and find out what happened. Eventually, the Red Cross gave us the information that both my grandfather and grandmother had been transported together on 13 July 1943, to Theresienstadt and then on 15 December 1943, to Auschwitz. They never returned.'

Doris feels that, even though her parents had escaped the worst under the Nazis, the tragedy had taken its toll on them. They died relatively early, in their sixties. Many of the relatives on her father's side perished also.

'I would like to find out more. My mother must have gone through hell, never knowing the fate of her parents. I know what it would have been like for me, not knowing if my parents were dead or alive. There was always this feeling that we had got away, but they didn't. It probably was a comfort to them that we had managed to get out, but when you think about it, here were these good, kind people, just minding their own business, not doing anyone any harm. They didn't deserve this fate.'

Doris still recalls the night back in 1938 when they left in a panic to escape the Nazis. 'Later, when I finally realised that I would never see my grandparents again, I remember breaking down in tears. They gave me presents. My grandfather gave me a gold amethyst ring, and my grandmother gave me a tortoiseshell hair brush. It was very sad. I was very close to my grandparents and I really regret that I had so little time with them. I have been really happy here in Ireland, but there are some times when I wonder what my life would have been if we did not have to leave our country.'

What Doris regrets most, apart from the loss of her relatives, is the fact that she also lost the warm family atmosphere she grew up with in her home town of Komotau. 'My uncle and his family went to Cardiff where they set up a spectacle frame company. My mother's cousin, Robert Heller and family, went to Israel and their sons went to England. Other cousins of my mother's went to Brazil and America, and others also to Wales and to London. All my family were split up.'

10

Rosel Siev

Downstairs in Rosel Siev's Rathgar home are the photographs of her children and her grandchildren, an affirmation of how life and happiness stretches out into the future. The past is lost, however, or partially locked away in an upstairs room, along with her private grief. Among the photographs she has kept hidden are those of her mother and father, who were killed by the Nazis. The photographs of her surviving sisters, Hilda, who escaped to Israel, and Hannelore, who was saved by Oskar Schindler, are the only ones she displays, even though they unleash memories of the tragic extermination of sixty-three members of her family during the war.

Until recently, Rosel Siev has never been able to talk about the Nazi period. 'I couldn't even tell my own children. We lost everything that was dear to us. It is very, very painful for me.' Her memories trigger off the nightmare which so often torments those who survived the Holocaust and still ask themselves why they were chosen for the perverse blessing of survival. 'Why me?' she asks. By what grotesque odds was Rosel Siev saved from the death camps which claimed so many other people in her family? By what odds was she destined, not only to bear the grief, but also the guilt of that silent, empty survival?

Since the war, Rosel Siev has married twice and has raised a family of six children, which must have somehow compensated, filling her house with the joy and thunder of new life. Her late, first husband, Arthur Goldstein of Manchester, encouraged her to put the war memories behind her, to live her life in England to the full with their two daughters, Carolyn and Sharon.

Since meeting and marrying the widowed solicitor Stanley Siev, she has been living in Dublin for the past twenty-two years, helping to rear his four children. 'My new family and my wonderful caring husband helped me to cope.' And Rosel Siev is an energetic woman, now in her seventies, speaking with a calm eloquence which still bears a slight trace of her German accent. At the back of her mind, however, lodge those terrible events both before and after 1939 when she was finally sent to England at the age of sixteen from her home in northern Germany.

Rosel (Wolff) Siev was born in 1921 in the small town of Aurich in Ost Friesland, close to the border with Holland. There were five children in the family: three girls and two boys. Her father, Martin Wolff, worked in the textile business. Rosel, the eldest, had always been a nervous and highly strung child and suffered most from the victimisation of Jews in school and elsewhere in their town after 1935.

'It was during the Hitler time, when I was fifteen, that I developed a serious throat infection. My throat closed up and I couldn't swallow anymore. I was studying in Frankfurt and staying with relatives at the time. They brought me to the nearest hospital, which happened to be a Catholic one. The nun in charge asked me my age, where I came from, and my religion. When I said I was Jewish, she put her hand on my shoulder and said: "My dear child, if we say you're Jewish, I don't know if you will come out alive. The doctors are Nazis in this hospital."

'The nun told me that my only hope was to put down my religion as Catholic. So I agreed. I was put on the trolley and wheeled into theatre. My relatives were sent away and here I was alone. It was in the middle of the night. The doors opened and in came a man, in brown

Hitler uniform, just throwing a white coat over him. I lay there and said to myself, my goodness here am I, a Jewish girl under the knife and a Nazi doctor operating on me. I just lay there praying and hoping.'

Rosel recovered, but her parents must have had some premonition of what was to happen under the Nazis in Germany and sent their eldest, most sensitive, daughter to relatives in England to study English. 'On the day they took me to the railway station, my parents must have realised they would never see me again. My sister Hanna told me after the war that the day I left was a black day, like Yom Kippur (the Jewish Day of Atonement). It was a very emotional departure as far as I can recollect, and I don't know how I got through it.'

In March 1942, she was informed through the Red Cross that her father had died in Buchenwald concentration camp. The last Rosel Siev heard from home was a message she received from her mother, Karoline Wolff, in May 1942 through the Red Cross.

The twenty-five words permitted in the message ran as follows: 'Before our journey we send greetings to you. We hope to see you again. Stay well and don't forget us – Hannelore, Wolfgang, Selly and Mutti.' After that it was absolute silence, just years and years of waiting. It was only much later that she realised that this 'journey' led to Lublin in Poland.

Rosel's sister Hilda managed to escape out of Germany in 1939 and reached Haifa after a traumatic journey that almost cost her her life. Between 1939 and 1940, Jewish refugees, mainly from Germany, Austria and Czechoslovakia, had reached Slovakia and had made their way in ships along the Danube and from the Black Sea to Palestine. None of them had visas and, on arrival in Palestine, they were interned. The British authorities then decided to deport a number of the refugees on a boat named the *Patria* to the island of Mauritius.

Rosel's sister Hilda was selected for deportation. The refugees protested and some of them blew up the ship to stop it from sailing.

The *Patria* sank with the loss of 250 Jewish lives. Hilda was among those who swam to shore where she was interned and transferred to a British prison camp in Atleit, Cyprus. After the war, she lived in Jerusalem and died in her sixties of leukemia.

'It emerged after the war from my surviving sister Hanna, that my mother and two young brothers were sent to Lublin in Poland where they had to work in quarries. My eldest brother, Wolfgang, disappeared in Majdeneck where my mother is also believed to have died. Hanna was sent to Auschwitz-Birkenau where she accidentally met our youngest brother, Selly, hardly recognisable.

'When she saw this boy of thirteen or fourteen, in rags, and very emaciated, she went over to him and asked, "Are you Selly Wolff?" It turned out that he was her brother. He was very ill and she tried to get him bread. I heard that when he was dying, he asked for her but the Nazi official wouldn't let her come to him. When we were reunited after the war in England, Hanna was unable to tell me this story. It was just too sad for her to relate. She told me this much later.'

Hannelore Wolff was taken to several different concentration camps before ending up fortuitously on Schindler's list. Recalling her tortuous journey through these camps, Hannelore (now Laura Hillman) composed a poem which is perhaps one of the most moving and vivid accounts of children in the death camp.

The Children of Auschwitz

I wake up at night
hear their cries
still
children,
always children
walking to the crematoria.

They carried their
dolls
teddybears
wide-eyed
or sleepy looking
bewildered
crying out
Mutti
Mama
Mamutchka
Mama
where have you gone?

Pink pajamas
blue nightgowns
fluffy dresses
shabby dresses
sailor suits
shoeless
unkempt
or neat looking
they walk by

I hear their measured steps
tramping on to the crematoria
watched by SS guards.
They rule their world now
had taken their mothers and
fathers away

And I hear the measured steps
tramping on and on
as geese flap their wings
and Nazis chase them
to stir up the wind.
Dust rising, blowing
the geese get louder
riding whips go
up and down.

But still
through the gaggling of the geese
I hear
the haunting cries of the children
of Auschwitz

The door of the crematoria is shut.
One last cry
Now silence.

Laura Hillman *(Courtesy of the Jewish Museum, Dublin)*

In Auschwitz, Hannelore eventually found herself standing in line for selection too. There was one line going straight to the gas-chambers, the other was a line of Jewish women who had been inadvertently sent to Auschwitz from the Plaszow camp near Cracow. Sensing that she was destined for death and that the other line meant a chance of hanging on to her life, Hannelore succeeded in slipping across unobserved by the guards from one line to the other. Only later did it come to light that there was one extra person on the Schindler line, but fortunately it she was not discovered by the guards and Hannelore escaped to Schindler's factory in Brunlitz, Czechoslovakia.

'Schindler was her saviour. Had she stayed in the other row, she would have gone into the showers to meet her end. I don't know why he allowed her to work for him. All that I know is that she was a very attractive girl. She had dark hair and a beautiful face. Hanna has written down all her recollections of her life, but I have never been able to read the manuscript. My husband advised me against it. It would be too upsetting. She called the book *Plant me a Lilac Tree*, which is a reference to the lilac tree my father once planted for my mother in Aurich.'

Oskar Schindler was the reluctant saviour of over 1,100 Jews in Cracow. The flawed hero who became the remarkable subject of Thomas Keneally's book and Stephen Spielberg's film *Schindler's List*, was known as much for his philandering and good living as for his extraordinary rescue of Jews. He had made his money on the black market in Cracow before taking over a confiscated enamelware factory and, like other German entrepreneurs, received permission to take Jewish workers from the Plaszow concentration camp, run by the notorious Amon Goeth. Schindler, a German Catholic businessman, retained cordial relations with the Gestapo throughout the war, allowing him not just to exploit his Jewish workers, but in the end also to protect them from being sent to their death.

By bribery and persuasion, Schindler kept Jewish workers employed in the production of kitchenware in the Cracow plant. He went out of his way to save entire families. In 1944, he relocated 500 of his workers to the Sudetenland, later adding another 700 to his list, claiming that these were skilled personnel who were needed for the production of munitions for the German war effort. Three hundred women on his list went missing and were transported to nearby Auschwitz instead of to his Brunlitz factory in the Sudetenland. Schindler then personally went to Auschwitz, bribing Nazi officials to allow him to take these women back to his plant to rejoin their families.

Close to the end of the war in January 1945, Oskar Schindler became aware of a locked goods wagon at the station near his armaments factory in Brunlitz. The wagon, marked property of the SS, was covered in ice and had been travelling for ten days. There were more than a hundred Jews inside, starving and frozen. While the official was distracted, Schindler quickly wrote on the transportation document that their final destination was for his factory in Brunlitz. He broke open the locks and found that sixteen of the occupants had already been frozen to death. The survivors also joined the Schindler Jews and were fed and nursed back to life by his wife Emilia.

Having been saved from death in Auschwitz, Hannelore Wolff met her future husband Bernard Hillman, a Czech, in Schindler's factory. Along with the normal rations of 100 grams of bread, a bowl of thin soup and two cups of ersatz coffee each day, Schindler managed to provide extra rations for his Jews. Bernard Hillman looked after Hannelore and since he worked in the kitchens, he did his best to get her extra food.

When Thomas Keneally was writing his book about Schindler, he contacted Hannelore to ask her about her experiences in Oskar Schindler's factory. She was still too distraught by what she had gone through to be able to discuss it at that time. Rosel Siev feels that Hannelore's husband, who is no longer alive, had also been badly affected by what had happened in the camps. 'My brother-in-law was very much an emotional casualty of the war. I don't know exactly what his tasks were, but I believe he had been informed that he had to carry out some horrendous tasks or failing that, he would be killed.

The Nazis gave him a terrible choice, and it certainly took its toll on him.'

'After the war in 1945, my sister married Bernard Hillman at a displaced person's camp in Munich. I kept the picture of their wedding upstairs. It was the most tragic picture that I've ever seen. A Jewish American army chaplain married them. She was in a black dress somebody had given her. He was wearing an old check jacket, a pair of trousers and a cap. They improvised the wedding canopy with a prayer shawl and four pieces of wood. It was an American soldier who had met my sister at this camp in southern Germany who phoned me at the Crumpsall Hospital in Manchester where I had qualified as a staff nurse. He had obtained my address from the Jewish Refugee Committee in England while he was on leave.'

Throughout the war, while Rosel waited to hear from Germany, she was considered as an enemy alien in Britain. In fact, most of the Jewish men who escaped to England were interned. The women were not, but there were many instances where they were required to report at regular intervals to police stations. 'Two of my mother's brothers, Abraham and Ludwig Wolff, escaped to England several days before the beginning of the war and where they were classed, like me, as enemy aliens. The menfolk who came over at that time were all interned on the Isle of Man and released only after several years.'

Rosel would not have been accepted to work in a munitions or arms factory, but she had to contribute to the war effort and opted to go into the nursing profession. However, the cruellest irony of the war was that, having escaped the worst horrors of the century, she was still regarded as an enemy in Britain. 'I found it very difficult to be accepted even as a nurse in England. There was absolutely no question of finding work. It was a matter of gaining admission for training as a nurse. All institutions were very wary of employing or taking on people with my background. They were very cagey, for England was at war and I was a German national. I don't think it was taken into consideration by people generally that Jews were being persecuted in Germany and that we were deprived of all our legal rights.'

Rosel was finally accepted and found work as a nurse in Crumpsall Hospital. During the war, the hospital was treating a group of badly injured German airmen and Rosel, being the only German-speaking nurse in the hospital, was ordered to take charge of the ward. She found these duties very difficult, but when the matron counselled her that nursing was beyond race or creed, Rosel put her reservations aside and accepted the Germans as normal patients. On one occasion, while treating one of these German soldiers, Rosel used a colloquial German Jewish expression, whereupon her patient called out to the rest of his comrades, warning them that she was a German Jewess and that they should beware of her.

'This was a horrible experience for me.' It was at this same hospital in 1946 that Rosel eventually got the message from an American soldier who had met Hannelore in a displaced persons camp outside Munich.

'He asked me was I Rosel Wolff. I said yes, and he told me that they had found my sister Hanna alive. He said she was very thin and quite ill, but she would be alright. I asked him if there was any news of the rest of my family, but he said they had found nobody else.

'Instead of coming to England as I had wished, Hanna and her husband decided to go to New York where he had relatives who were willing to act as their guarantors. They went to America without a penny, and a very kind doctor took Hanna in hand and treated her. She had many operations for gall bladder and thyroid. She also had diabetes, but ultimately she was cured.'

Rosel then married in England, and her first husband sent a ticket to her sister Hannelore in New York as well as to her sister Hilda in Palestine to come over to England for a reunion. In 1951, the three sisters finally met again, eleven or twelve years after they had parted. 'I went down to Southampton to meet Hanna. I was expecting to see an undernourished, completely emaciated girl. As I waited at six in the morning with an armful of roses, I saw her coming down from the boat in the shadow of a Catholic nun who took care of her on the ship. Here I saw a girl looking exactly like Audrey Hepburn, wearing a huge picture hat and absolutely beautifully groomed. I couldn't believe it was my sister. She was very thin, but she looked wonderful.'

'We went by train to London, and from London to Manchester. It seemed like an endless journey. We had so much to talk about. But I don't think I could take it all in at that stage. Then she met Hilda and the three of us were together in my home in Manchester. I was twenty-eight, Hilda was twenty-six and Hanna was twenty-five.'

In Dublin, Rosel Siev has since been persuaded mostly by her children that, because she is living testimony to the Holocaust, she has a duty to record her memories. 'Now that I have time on my hands, all this process is going through my mind. These memories recur again and again, and I am preoccupied with the thoughts of what happened to us. I have been deprived of my most precious possessions, my beloved parents, my family, my youth, my education. I was never bitter, but I will never forget and I will never be able to forgive. I'm no Gordon Wilson. The Nazis subjected me to a life of passive torture that will stay with me until the end of my days.'

11

Helen Lewis

At a very early age in Belfast, Helen Lewis's two sons, Michael and Robin, began to ask about the tattoo on her arm bearing the number BA677. She told them she would explain it later, when they were older and would understand. And inevitably, by the age of nine or ten, the boys discovered all about the concentration camps, about the selections, and the gas chambers at Auschwitz and Stutthof.

They learned how their Czech-born mother, had received the tattoo and signed a document stating that she was to be kept at Auschwitz-Birkenau for an undisclosed period of time, after which she would undergo *Sonderbehandlung* (special treatment) by order of the *Reichsfuehrer*. They learned how she had survived many times over, how she was saved once by virtue of her talents as a dancer and choreographer, and how she was eventually taken on one of the infamous winter death marches in the closing days of the war. They learned how close their mother had come to death before she escaped by throwing herself into a snow-filled ditch and finally made her long way back to Prague, and later to Belfast.

Perhaps it was telling her extraordinary story to her children that shaped the way Helen Lewis was to recall these events without the slightest trace of rancour or bitterness. It was not for herself, but for them that she ultimately put those memories into words. When they were older, her sons asked her to write down the details; not for publication but for the next generation. Eventually, she began to find time here and there to put down the facts – memories which had cast aside any notion of blame or judgement; memories distilled by time into the clear and objective view of her survival and the destruction of life around her. Later, encouraged by writers Michael Longley and Jennifer Johnston, she continued to write a most remarkable autobiography under the title *A Time to Speak*.

It is not just the story of endurance, how she and other inmates coped with desperate conditions, working for sixteen hours a day with the constant threat of death if they slacked or showed any weakness. It also tells of the kindness of a camp guard, of essential camp friendships, of betrayal, and of how frail the will to survive can become in isolation. For Helen Lewis, survival is not bound together with any sense of virtue, only fate. Perhaps it is also due to the positive thread which runs through her life, but she feels it is unfair to the memory of others who did not come out alive, to connect her endurance with any personal attributes or strength of will. 'People say God protected me. Does that mean he didn't protect those who died? I am totally unable to answer those questions. It was often a matter of timing: a fortnight later, I would not have been alive.'

The personal story of Helen Lewis now seems to speak for all the others who didn't make it. 'I believe the truth must come out. There are survivors who refuse to say anything to their children, and I think it is very, very wrong to react that way. Children don't ask out of curiosity, they ask because it concerns them. If we don't tell what happened, it puts the next generation into a very awkward position. It will generate dark spots of ignorance and doubt.'

Today, Helen Lewis lives and works in Belfast as a well-known choreographer for theatre and opera, having founded the Belfast Modern Dance Group and rebuilt a life in the arts which had been denied her by the Nazis. Dance not only saved her on one occasion from death in Stutthof concentration camp, but also from the trauma of her memories afterwards. 'It saved me from the psychological torment which so many other survivors have experienced.' In 1947, Helen Lewis moved to Belfast after she had married Harry Lewis, an old friend from her home town of Trutnov. He had escaped to Belfast at the start of the war.

Her previous marriage is like a journey through the Holocaust, from which she returned while her first husband, Paul, did not. They were taken to Theresienstadt and on to Auschwitz where they were separated. She never saw him again. He died in Schwarzheide concentration camp just before the end of the war; the last card from him was dated 15 March 1945.

Born in the picturesque border town of Trutnov in the Sudetenland, steeped in German culture, Helen Lewis was brought up in a comfortable home where poetry, music and opera had an important place. At the age of six, she decided to devote her life to dance, much to the amusement of her teachers and friends. Later on, a romance with Harry Lewis came to an end when she chose to pursue dance as a professional career. After the death of her father, Helen and her mother, who supported her ambitions as a dancer, moved to Prague, where she studied dance and married her first husband, Paul. Soon afterwards, however, the first signs of tragedy for the country came with the Munich Conference. And on 15 March 1939, Helen, Paul and her mother listened to the news on the radio that Czechoslovakia had summarily been declared a protectorate of the Third Reich under Hitler. There were German tanks on the streets of Prague.

The magnitude of this development had a shattering effect on the family when Helen's cousin and her husband, who had witnessed the persecution of Jews in Germany in the 30s, jumped from their fifth floor apartment and were found dead in the street. Many young people left the country. But for Helen and Paul, emigration would have meant leaving behind her mother and his parents which was out of the question. They opted to stay in Prague. Letters home also confirmed how lonely and rejected people felt after leaving. And in any case, the future didn't look too bad yet.

But the situation became steadily worse as the anti-Jewish laws were promulgated, jobs were lost, bank accounts were frozen, property confiscated and Jews were forbidden to take part in the life of the city and the country. After war was declared, Helen recalls the feeling of relief in Prague when people mistakenly believed the Germans would hold out only for a matter of months. Her mother was evicted from her flat in a district which Germans coveted. All Jews were required to register at the Central Jewish Office. All Jews over the age of six had to wear a yellow star. Each new directive seemed like the worst one possible.

Among the personal possessions which Jews had to hand over to the authorities were not only their radios, jewellery and valuables, but also their pets. Helen Lewis recalls how for many people this became the cruellest blow. Not knowing what was yet to come, people travelled in shock on the trams with their white mice, tortoises, guinea pigs and caged birds. 'Dogs and cats were the worst. They cried all the way, as if they knew.' And Helen recounts in her book how Paul's father looked devastated after he brought his much-loved canary, Pepicek, to the animal collection centre.

Inevitably, it seems, they waited for the next step, and in 1941 the register of Jews in Prague led the way to the first deportations. Each deportee was permitted to take 50 kilos of luggage and they were ordered to leave their homes and belongings behind in immaculate condition for the new German owners. With the uncertain future, Helen recalls how people agonised over what few possessions to take with them, whether to bring practical belongings like bedclothes or cooking utensils, or to bring precious photographs, books, or family objects that were dear to them. Every day, people were seen on the streets and trams hauling their luggage to the official assembly point at the Trade Fair hall.

Postcards began to come back from Theresienstadt and Lodz; thirty permitted words which initially confirmed that everyone was 'fine', but later included coded messages pleading for food. Other more sinister messages came from friends who described themselves as widows; for Helen and Paul came the news that a certain friend had disappeared.

Very soon it was Paul's parents who received the summons for deportation. Then it was Helen's mother's turn. 'I only know that nothing that followed was as painful as parting from her, letting her go while I had to stay behind.' Unable even to accompany her mother to the assembly point, Helen resigned herself to the fact that sooner or later, their names would also come up. A short while after, she heard that her mother had been transported to a camp near Lublin in Poland and it was almost with relief that in August 1942, Helen and her husband Paul eventually received the summons too. Bidding farewell to their friends, they played Dvorak's Cello Concerto on the gramaphone, wept and embraced. They did not know that they would never hear that music together again.

Arriving in Theresienstadt by train, followed by a two and a half hour march in the sun, they were left for hours without water or food before eventually being housed in barracks. There was hunger all around, and the food, which had seemed so tasteless at first, became essential. Helen was sent to work looking after children. Some time later, she met a respected conductor by the name of Raphael Schaechter who had undertaken to perform Smetana's opera *The Bartered Bride* and was looking for a choreographer.

At the Theresienstadt ghetto, designed to house 3,000 and eventually swelling to 50,000 people, there was still room for music, drama and dance. Indeed, it brought together a thriving artistic community to which Helen contributed until she became ill with acute appendicitis. Under the circumstances, she received the best treatment from doctors and nurses who were prisoners like herself. Around that time, news had come from Prague to say that her mother was in Sobibor camp, a fact which filled Helen with hope at first. But as one transport after another left for the unknown, the sense of hope began to diminish. Helen and Paul were eventually sent to on to Auschwitz where they were divided into groups of men and women and marched under the gateway bearing the sign: *Arbeit macht frei.*

Birkenau, a sub-camp of Auschwitz, made the soul-destroying deprivations of Theresienstadt seem a lot less harsh; the terror of the new conditions was registered on everyone's face. It was here that Helen again met Mitzi, an acquaintance whom she had known from Theresienstadt, and as the initial shock of Birkenau sank in, they sealed a companionship which was to last for three years through the camps.

From time to time, as new transports kept arriving in Birkenau, people who had already been there for some time would be taken away for extermination in the gas-chambers. Sometimes there were delays, but also rumours and confusion, which increased the fear among inmates. Those who were to die were selected from rows of naked inmates carrying their bundles of clothes to be individually inspected by the notorious Nazi doctor, Joseph Mengele. Anyone with physical blemishes went through a doorway to their death, while those who were deemed perfect went through a different door to a life of forced labour.

Because Helen had been operated on in Theresienstadt, she bore a mass of red scars on her stomach. She felt doomed, but passed the first selection when, after hours, the camp guards became impatient and ordered the prisoners to keep their clothes on. Three days later, in another selection, she found herself standing in the long queues of naked women. But this time, with armed guards all around, she took a huge risk, stepped out of her queue and joined the queue of women who had already passed. Afterwards, she was overjoyed to meet Paul, who had also passed his selection, though they would not be together for long because he was soon sent away to a work camp in Germany, never to be seen again.

The women who passed the selections were transferred from the family camp to the women's camp and on the same night, the sky 'lit up in a profusion of colours from bright orange to deep red' as they watched the fire which consumed those who had been left behind, including Paul's mother. Finally, there was yet one more unbearable selection before Helen was sent on to Stutthof concentration camp near the Baltic Sea in Poland where they had to work under extreme conditions, forced to battle with the cold. There were few bunks, little or no blankets and only the minimum of food. They spent sixteen hours a day building an airfield, all the time watched by camp guards eager to spot signs of weakness which would result in them being sent to the Stutthof gas-chamber and incinerators. Helen recalls how under these conditions, the shovel alone felt like a huge weight in her hands. Her book captures the essential nature of friendship during this time.

> Friendship in the camps meant sharing in every sense. The little bit of space, the little bit of food, the moments of acute danger and the occasional laughter. We gradually came to understand that this type of friendship was based on necessity first and on affection afterwards. To have a friend meant to have an extra pair of eyes to spot approaching danger, a voice to warn and a pair of hands to support you when in need.
>
> *A Time to Speak*

To Helen Lewis, the SS guards symbolised a perversion of humanity, but sometimes, in rare situations, the odd one one showed kindness and extraordinary compassion. One young SS woman once noticed how weak Helen had become and had a fire lit where they sat and exchanged their life stories. Later, the SS woman, whose name was Traute, gave Helen some medication for dysentery. There was another SS man, a former teacher, who saved part of his own food rations each day to give to one of the prisoners. Towards the end of the war, he went on to keep the remaining sick and dying inmates alive with food and medicine. It was these inmates who in turn spoke up for him when the Russians arrived, insisting that he should go free.

Ultimately, the awful conditions continued to take their toll and Helen became weaker and weaker. She was close to death when her reputation as a dancer and choreographer came to the attention of the woman commander, who then saw to it that she was given extra rations. She was nursed back to reasonable health so that she could help to stage the most bizarre Christmas show by choreographing *Valse from Coppelia*. Dancing with her frost-bitten feet became her only path back to life. She managed to get her friend Mitzi a job as a seamstress for the costumes. Right up until Christmas they were fed extra rations, but then they were returned to the original hardship.

By early 1945, the Russian army was already very close to Stutthof, and many of the able inmates were taken on what became known as the 'death march'. For weeks, they had to walk along icy roads in 'ever decreasing circles'. Many of the SS travelled ahead in a horse-drawn cart. The SS shouted at the prisoners, shooting anyone who lagged behind. At one stage, they were forced to stay in a barn which quickly turned to unbearable squalor, with lice and dysentery. The dead and dying were lined up in a heap at the door. Helen became withdrawn and isolated.

> One morning I took my blanket and without a word went to lie down among the dying. I pulled the blanket over my face and gave up. A few of the girls who saw me lying there tried to talk to me, but when I did not react, they sighed, then shrugged, and finally stopped trying . . . From time to time I became aware of myself and my situation, but more often I was lost in fantasies.
>
> One evening, like a sleepwalker, I got up, took my blanket and climbed painfully back to my former place. I had had no blinding revelation, no inner voice had talked to me, no gentle hand that guided me, and yet I had got up and gone back among the living.
>
> *A Time to Speak*

The same night, the living were forced to move on, stumbling through the bitter cold. Helen lost the support of Mitzi, who had been persuaded by others in their group that it was useless to try and save her, and that Helen would only drag them down to their doom. At one point along the death march, Mitzi allowed Helen's hand to slip out of her grasp. For Helen, on her own now, it would have meant certain death but for the fact that she took a chance to save herself. Seeing that the march had momentarily stopped close to a house, and that there was a snow-covered ditch beside them, she jumped in. When the 'death march' moved on, she pulled herself out of the snow and went into the house where German soldiers gave her food and a place to lie down. Suffering from typhoid and running a terrible fever, she was eventually found by a major of the liberating Russian army who cared for her and finally gave her a small piece of paper on which he had scribbled his name and rank, entreating people to look after her.

'That Russian soldier was my Schindler. The idea was that my book should tell the truth. And it has turned out that the most humane people were sometimes the most unlikely ones, like some SS guards. Why not give them the right to let their story be known as well? If they were decent, why not say it? The book is a tribute to these people.'

With this note from the Russian officer, Helen managed to get to a Red Cross hospital and begin the slow road to recovery and back to Prague. At home, she discovered how her husband Paul had died in Schwarzheide, so close to the end of the war. She had also discovered a curious story of how Mitzi, her former camp friend, had related the last days on the 'death march', telling everyone how she had held Helen in her arms as she died. Inevitably, Helen met Mitzi again in Prague, but the original friendship could never be restored.

In October 1945, Helen got a postcard from 'that faraway city in foreign lands, called Belfast'. It had been written by her friend Harry Lewis, who had spotted her name among the Red Cross list of survivors. They got married in Prague in June 1947 and moved to Belfast where she feels very much at home. 'I have very warm feelings for Belfast. It was an incredibly fruitful time for me here. It was a case of being in the right place at the right time. When it came to dance, Belfast just had classical and Irish dancing up to then, and they were ready for something new. I was there at the right moment and was given so many opportunities.'

Helen feels very fortunate also to have got out of Prague and to have escaped the misery and oppression of the communist regime which took hold of the country after the war. People now often ask her why she still lives in Belfast with the troubles, and in many ways, she has become a symbol of the pluralist society which Irish society has not quite yet reached.

'Like everybody else, I would like the troubles to be over. They appal me and I can't understand them to this day. I like people to recognise and respect the differences in each other and to feel that people are more interesting because they are different. I fear and intensely dislike the kind of fundamentalism which arises in all religions. It seems totally nonsensical. To me, what has been happening in Northern Ireland is very, very sad.'

Her years with Harry and their two children were filled with great happiness. He came around to the idea of dance, supporting her in every way. They often laughed at the arguments they had had back in Czechoslovakia over her dance career. As Helen was writing her book, Harry would type it up for her, though sadly, he never lived to see its publication.

Initially, after she arrived in Belfast, putting the trauma of those years in the concentration camps behind her, Helen used to have nightmares. In spite of the warmth and security of her homelife, she suffered these regular horrors at night from which she would wake up screaming. 'For hours afterwards I would be in a dreadful state. The dreams were always the same and connected with the death camps. The interesting thing is that I've never had one of these nightmares since my first child was born. It may sound a bit corny, but somehow life defeated death. Giving birth, giving life to a lovely, healthy child, gave me roots and peace of mind.'

12

Geoffrey Phillips

Geoffrey Phillips (originally Günther Philipps) was eight years old when Hitler came to power in Germany. He was the only son of a butcher in the small town of Wanne-Eickel, about fifteen miles from Dortmund and went to school through the early years of Nazi oppression. He witnessed the swift demoralisation of Jews in the town and saw his father's thriving business ruined. One day, just before Christmas 1938, along with several thousand other German children, he was sent away by his parents on what has become known perhaps as the most heartbreaking of all journeys of that time: the *Kindertransport*. He didn't even know where he was going. He had a small suitcase, as well as another little bag with provisions and a ticket to a foreign land. He never saw his parents alive again. He was barely thirteen.

Geoffrey Phillips now lives in Blackrock, County Dublin. He and his wife Phyllis moved there from Bradford almost forty years ago, when Geoffrey opened a textile firm. Now, Geoffrey Phillips is still trying to piece together the tragedy of his family. Just after the war, he made his way back to his home-town as a British soldier, but left again when he was told that his parents had been killed and when he discovered that the very people who had been in the Nazi Party were still running the civil administration in Wanne-Eickel alongside the Allies. He was so upset at the time that he got on the first train out of the town and when he got back to Bradford he destroyed all his letters and most of his photographs; every connection with his home and family. Only now has he begun to allow his memories to bring it all back again.

In the intervening years, he has spoken very little about his experiences, even to his wife, who is now hearing many details of his childhood for the first time. He resolved never to return to his hometown again. Now, in his sixties, Geoffrey Phillips has agreed to accept an invitation from the municipal authorities who, as a gesture of reconciliation, have asked the former Jewish citizens to revisit their native town.

'Hitler and his Nazi party seized power in January 1933. To begin with, they dealt with their political opponents, mainly the communists and socialists, and the Jews were left alone. But in April of that year, the first blow fell, when the Nazis staged a nationwide boycott of all Jewish businesses. Brownshirts would stand in front of our shop with placards saying, "Don't buy from Jews". It was all imposed officially. I think the reaction of most people was that it would last for a short while and then things would go back to normal.'

In the small town of Wanne-Eickel, people tried to lead as normal a life as possible under the circumstances. However, they learned otherwise when the Nazis announced their programme which aimed at the elimination of Jews from the economic and cultural life of Germany. All Jews holding public positions, such as teachers, judges, doctors and actors lost their jobs. In the case of private businesses, such as the Phillips' butcher shop, their non-Jewish customers may first have continued as before, but gradually the intimidation and constant repetition of anti-semitic propaganda had their effect. People would not risk their careers by being seen coming out of Jewish shops and, by degrees, most of the non-Jewish customers fell away. It became progressively harder to make a living.

The irony was that in Wanne-Eickel, as in most other places in Germany, the Jews had integrated totally into their host society. The ancestors of the Phillips family had lived in Westphalia and the Rhineland since the time of Napoleon.

'Prior to Hitler coming, the only difference between my family and the others in the town is that they went to a Catholic or Protestant church and we went to a synagogue. We had slightly different holidays and so on. Otherwise we were totally accepted. My father was a German soldier in the First World War, as was my uncle. They were both members of the old veterans association and in general joined in everything in the town.'

The rise of Hitler cleared the way for hundreds of official strategies in which the Jews could suddenly be discriminated against. At school, for example, Geoffrey recalls the humiliation and violence directed at Jewish children.

'The normal thing was for a child to go to the Jewish elementary school and then on to the secondary school. By the time I was ten and old enough to go, any of the Jewish students that were still there had special seats reserved for them at the back of the class. No matter how clever they were, they failed or only barely passed their exams. Many teachers actively encouraged physical violence against Jewish students. Our school was on a quiet side street, five minutes walk away from home. We always had to walk in groups of five or six, because if you were on your own, you might end up getting stones thrown at you or getting a good hiding.'

With his father's business going down, it was increasingly difficult to pay the school fees. Jews were shunned by everyone, even friends and colleagues. In private, people still acknowledged that they did not agree with Nazi thinking, but in public they had to be seen to have nothing to do with Jews.

'Progressively things became worse and justice became totally perverted. One incident sticks in my mind. It was soon impossible for a Jew to own a motor car and so they would have to travel around on bicycles. One day, this Jewish man was out on his bike and he must have been recognised, because a car drove at him at great speed. He swerved and got his bicycle wheel caught in the tramlines. As it happened, the tram was coming along and had to stop to avoid running him over. Afterwards, he was prosecuted and sentenced to three months in jail for causing a public disturbance by obstructing the progress of the tram.

'I know of another man who owned a hire purchase business, and they had him marched around the town with a placard around his neck saying, "I'm a Jewish bloodsucker who exploits poor Germans," and again he was prosecuted for causing a public disturbance. Incidents like that happened all over.'

In the end, Geoffrey's father had to sell the business. And because it had been run down to such a degree over four years, an arbitrator was called in to evaluate it and to decide on a knock down price. In 1936, when Germany held the Olympic Games in Berlin and wanted to show foreigners that things were not so bad, there was a temporary improvement. But as soon as the Games were over, everything changed again and new anti-Jewish laws were issued regularly. One of these was that all male Jews had to add 'Israel' and females 'Sarah' to additional forenames and these had to appear on all official correspondence and documents. Passports were overstamped with a huge red J. Another law required all Jews to submit itemised lists of their possessions and valuables, down to belongings such as wedding rings. Finally on 9 November 1938, the Nazis began closing down all Jewish businesses and burning down the synagogues.

'That was *Kristallnacht*. In the early hours of the morning we heard that our synagogue had been set on fire by squads of Hitler Youth. Later on we heard that same thing was happening all over the country. Before we had recovered from the shock of this terrible news, there was a knock on the door. Two plain clothes policeman asked for my father, told him to pack a change of clothes and took him away. Subsequently, we heard that everywhere the heads of Jewish households had been arrested.

'Fortunately, the local police still followed normal protocol; they were not rough in any way. In other towns the roundup was conducted by the SS, which would have made it quite a different matter. We heard afterwards that my father had been taken into a concentration camp.

'A cousin of my father's was the welfare officer of the Jewish community in a neighbouring town; through her, we heard that as a consequence of *Kristallnacht*, the people of Britain and Holland were going to take in a limited number of young children from Germany and Austria. The cousin urged my mother: "You must get your boy registered for this transport."'

On 15 December 1938, after a heartbreaking farewell, Geoffrey left his family, hoping that some day they might all be reunited. The train took him to the assembly point, where many more children from the area had been collected. They boarded the special carriages of the *Kindertransport* which took about 200 children over the Dutch border to the Hook of Holland and from there by ferry-boat to Harwich. 'All in all there were several thousand, some from Vienna, some from Berlin, some from Hamburg. On arrival in England, they separated the boys and the girls.

'Most of the boys like myself finished up in a holiday camp near Lowestoft, which was normally closed down at that time of the year but which now accommodated nearly a thousand boys. It was close to Christmas, one of the coldest winters ever and there was a foot and a half of snow on the ground. The pipes froze. In the end they had to move us out of there because we didn't even have water to wash. So they put us into a couple of ballrooms in hotels. Our group finished up in a swanky public school for girls near Southwold in Suffolk. The girls left funny messages for us, things like "I hope you will be very hot in my bed". When the winter holidays ended, we had to clear out again and were sent to another holiday camp in Harwich. We moved around, here, there and everywhere. Finally, I ended up in Bradford where the Jewish community together with other groups put together sufficient money to buy a big house which was converted into a hostel for boys. There were twenty-four of us.'

Geoffrey and his companions went to special classes to learn English. Otherwise, he had not been in school since the day before he had left Germany. Bradford was a well-known textile manufacturing town and when the war broke out, Geoffrey was sent to work a mill, rolling cloth, a job he describes as 'filthy'. 'We started work at 6:45 every morning and finished at 5:30 in the evening.'

In the first letter from home he learned that his father had been released and returned to Wanne-Eickel a few days after Geoffrey had left Germany. Prior to the outbreak of war, he and his parents could write freely to each other, although they had to be careful what they wrote because much of the mail was opened by the Germans. The last letter was obviously conveying a farewell message and included the words: 'God bless you and keep you.'

'I kept all their letters in a box. But when I found out what happened to them, I just chucked the whole bloody lot out. This was after I'd gone over to look for my parents. There are people who don't want to talk about it. When you get to know the details, like how close my parents were to being rescued, but through the avarice or dishonesty of someone else that fell apart, you feel disconsolate. It seems that the only way to lead a normal life is to shut it all out. You have the alternative of keeping it at bay, by not talking about it, or like others reliving it every day.'

Still hoping to find his parents alive and well, Geoffrey Phillips volunteered for the British army in 1943 and joined an infantry unit. 'The human mind always preserves some little spark of hope. I thought that by some miracle somebody might have survived.' His unit was sent to a region north of Bremen, rounding up and sorting out what was left of the German army and supervising their disbandment. In 1945 with Germany's infrastructure in ruins, it was difficult to find out anything about his parents. Gradually about the time that the railways started to work again, he got a message from a former schoolmate that she and her mother had got back from a camp in Poland. In July, Geoffrey applied for compassionate leave and went back to his home-town.

'I met this girl and her mother whose brother and father had been killed. They were taken away at the same time as my parents, first to the ghetto in Riga where they were kept for some time. Every so often they had selections, people who were taken from the ghetto. The Germans had invented fiendish methods to fill these transports, putting Jews in charge. The *Judenrat* (Jewish Committee) would be told, "We want four hundred people, it's up to you to get them. We want them two days from now at 8 o'clock in the morning." It was understood that if there were not four hundred, if there were only three hundred and ninety-six, then they would take four members from a *Judenrat* family. This put a huge moral strain on these committee members. It was as if they had to pronounce a death sentence on their own people. A lot of these people, who were used for this purpose, killed themselves; they just couldn't take it.

'Eventually it came to my own family's turn. My father, my mother, a maiden aunt, a bachelor uncle. My mother was selected first. But then my Aunt Julia volunteered to go instead of her so that my parents could stay together. I think it was very heroic of her. Where my family went to, nobody knows.

'I only had a few details. But I didn't want to find out anymore. It was irrelevant where they were sent. The result was the same. They never came back. I felt so miserable and depressed that I went down to the station and found that there was a goods train leaving at 9 o'clock that evening. I picked up my kit bag and put it into the guards van. I just wanted to get out of the town. I didn't want to spend another night there.

'From what I heard afterwards, of a total Jewish population of approximately one hundred deported from my home-town, there were only ten left. On average only ten per cent of Jews in Germany managed to survive. This is not counting the ones who left before the war, but those who were hidden by friends or survived the camps. Even the efficiency of the German technology did not manage to exterminate all Jews.

'What was even more depressing was the news of my parents' near escape. Former neighbours told me how unlucky they had been, almost managing to get out. A cousin of my mother's living in

Washington, had deposited money with an agency in Colombia or Equador to purchase my family's entry visas in that country. My parents had gone as far as getting their furniture sold and were buying things they could take with them. One day, I received a letter from South America from someone who had been acting as go-between for my American relatives and my parents. The money for my parents' visas was accidentally sent to the wrong official who absconded with it.

'If the people in South America had played it straight, there was a very good chance that my parents would have managed to get out of Germany before the deportations started. Lots of German and Austrian Jews finished up in those countries; some of them or their descendants are still there. My parents would have survived.'

Having discovered that he had lost four close members of his family, Geoffrey Phillips became so disheartened that he could no longer spend any more time in his town. What fuelled his utter dejection at the time was the discovery that nothing had changed. The war had ended, the Allies had wrestled Germany back from Nazi fear, and still the same people were in charge of his town. There had been show trials in Nuremberg but, otherwise, the key positions of Nazi supporters during the war had not been vacated. The absolute obedience to the Führer had merely shifted to obedience to the British army.

He wondered why he had volunteered for the army. Who had they liberated? Here were the people who had collaborated in the deportation of his family. While he was in Wanne-Eickel to find out what had become of his parents, after a conversation with a sergeant major of the British army, he was told it was official policy that the rank and file German officials were to be kept in place. He was shown the filing cabinets containing the information on each and every Nazi member, though the British had been instructed not to take any action. It is significant that not one member of the judiciary from the Nazi era has ever been prosecuted in relation to Nazi war crimes.

'They wanted to get the Germans on our side, because there was a fear that the whole of Germany might end up in Russian hands and turn communist, like Poland and East Germany. So this process of de-Nazification was stopped. There was also a pragmatic element; because these Nazis knew how to run the show, what was the point in putting all of them behind barbed wire when they were helping to run Germany? They wanted to get the civil administration going again.

'So the Nazi members kept their posts and were happy to work with the British army of occupation, just to save their skin. When you see an almighty cover-up like that going on, naturally it gets to you. Forget about justice and retribution, all for the sake of political expediency. Politics dictated, and yesterday's enemy became today's friend.'

When Geoffrey Phillips and his infantry unit were quartered in a village near Cuxhaven, he discovered the *burgermeister* (mayor) of the village was a true Nazi. 'When I went into his office, there was still a picture of Hitler hanging on the wall. I made him take it down and smashed it up in front of him. "Oh yes," he said, "I'd forgotten about that." He was still there acting as mayor. Very dutifully, he offered to do anything we wanted.'

Geoffrey Phillips had become totally disillusioned. Two days after his twenty-first birthday, he returned to Britain and went back to his job as a loom tuner in Bradford. He worked his way up through the harsh conditions of the British textile industry, getting up every morning before 6 a.m. Like many of the other children who had been sent away on the *Kindertransport*, he worked very hard, and eventually reached a managerial position in his firm. At the local synagogue youth group, he met his wife Phyllis and they got married. In 1951, they moved to Ireland, where Geoffrey set up a textile factory in Sallynoggin, County Dublin. They have three grown up sons, David, Jonathan and Robert.

'I have told my children very little. It is very difficult. But this is not untypical of those who have come through the same experience as myself. It's like somebody wanting to slam the door on the whole chamber of horrors and throw away the key. I know of several people who have gone through far more harrowing experiences than myself and if anybody asks them to participate in any kind of recollection the answer is always a categorical "no". They don't want to be reminded. It's too hard for them to even think about it.

'I myself have got through this. I didn't want to forget, nor could I forget. My attitude is that I'm happy that our three boys could grow up as free people and didn't have go through the same experiences as I did. They had all kinds of friends, Jews, Catholics and Protestants. When we lived in Killiney, they were in the cubs and in the boy scouts. They could do things which I could never do as a child. We used to put all the cubs into the factory lorry and take them to Greystones for a picnic. They all had tremendous fun. So why dig all this out? How can a young child understand all this?'

In 1988, the children who had been sent on the *Kindertransport* in 1938, held a reunion in the hostel in Bradford which had since been turned into a hotel. Geoffrey feels there was certain catharsis in this meeting and has since become a member of a group called 'the children of the transport'. 'We can talk about it together without feeling that we are scratching at an old wound.

'Yes, it was hard and lonely. After all there was a complete wall of silence between us and our folks back at home. We could only guess at what was happening. Most of us felt that we had to literally pull ourselves up by our boot-straps, to educate ourselves. Nobody said you have to go to nightschool. If we wanted to make something of our own lives, we had to do it ourselves; we had no parents or near relations to guide us or to encourage us.'

Geoffrey Phillips can talk about the past, though not altogether dispassionately. His wife Phyllis confirms that now is the first time in his life that he can discuss the subject without crying. His memories are still raw and it takes quite an effort; he finds himself bringing to mind things he had forgotten, or thought he had forgotten. 'If you want to tell it properly, in some respects it means reliving it again.'

Afterword

There remains very little which can be said that might add to the voices of those I have interviewed for this book. Nothing could ever match the potency of their original testimony, or the dignity with which they recall their years of isolation and loss. Indeed, I was struck many times by their extraordinary presence, as though the rest of us were mere shadows of their strength and abiding endurance, as though the merest contact instantly causes our own mundane battles with life to disappear. I can only hope that this book will have passed on the experience and the great privilege of meeting them and witnessing their courage.

Since writing *Hidden Memories*, I have found myself looking around at all kinds of gatherings: at dinner with family members; at parties with friends; even at a funeral where it was brought home to me how these social rituals, which essentially support us through our lives, were brutally denied to so many people during the Holocaust. All the fixed social markers, which we take for granted, disappeared; all the intimacies and all the safety on which we build our lives. I found myself imagining the sudden loss of these personal beacons and all the people I know. I found myself staring at friends and relatives, thinking what it could have been like to be so suddenly cut off from them. I felt the terror at the involuntary thought of what might have happened to them. Like Suzi Diamond and many other survivors, no doubt, I could not help wondering who would have made it, who would have survived and who would have died, until I am reminded once more of how grotesque the Nazi extermination process actually was. I then asked myself: Why should anyone have to prepare for such a calamity? Why should anyone have to assume that such degradation and fear could be normal? Why should anyone be denied their friends, their parents, children, husbands, wives in such a deliberate way?

The fact that these survivors and witnesses have given us an account of the unspeakable is remarkable in itself. For many of them, it would have been impossible to have approached the subject in a public way at a younger age. We are deeply indebted to them for imparting these first-hand accounts and for giving us that vital information, which may protect us and future generations from allowing such atrocities to occur again. Their words have ensured that we can never be complacent or self-obsessed. In a way, they have made sure that we always remain conscious of others, always vigilant.

For those survivors and witnesses in this book, much of the impulse to speak has to do with the fact that they are older now, and that they have brought up their own children. With a half a century between us and the events of the Nazi era, what links them is a dedication and belief that their children and grandchildren can in some ways put everything right again. Like Rosel Siev, many still feel, under that positive outward expression, the instinctive guilt at their own survival. As for Helen Lewis, the sense of healing has come through the young, forcing a distillation of the process of memory into a vivid narrative recollection, without hate or vengeance. It has not diminished the horror of those memories, or the range of emotions. But it has helped the survivors to cope and renew their faith in the next generations.

For Rosel Siev, as for Zoltan Zinn-Collis and Suzi Diamond, this is what has prompted them to break their self-enforced silence. It has become clear that very few of the people speaking out in this book ever knew of each other's experiences before. Even though for Jack and Solly Steinberg, the loss of their sister is part of the horrific events in Nazi Europe, their grief has always remained deeply private. In effect, the survivors of the Holocaust have become even more isolated by their intense suffering. It is not something we can easily speak about every day.

For Sabina Shorts, Doris Segal and Geoffrey Phillips, there has never been a reason to come together to discuss the past. By the nature of things, the Holocaust memory is not a convivial subject. It was as though the Holocaust had always inadvertently consigned each and everyone to their own silence. *Hidden Memories* should mark our way of supporting them in their private suffering, a way of acknowledging their existence in Ireland. I hope this book has helped to end that silence and that it will stand as a recognition of their personal tragedy. It is a tribute to them.

Selected Bibliography

Bielenberg, Christabel: *The Past is Myself* (Chatto and Windus, 1968)

Collis, Robert: *To Be a Pilgrim* (Secker & Warburg, 1975)

Collis, Robert and Han Hogerzeil: *The Lost and the Found* (Women's Press, New York 1953)

Collis, Robert and Han Hogerzeil: *Straight On* (Methuen, 1947)

Fest, Joachim: *The Face of the Third Reich* (Penguin, 1972)

Fisher, David and Anthony Read: *Berlin: The Biography of a City* (Hutchinson, 1994)

Frank, Anne: *The Diary of Anne Frank* (Pan, 1954)

Gilbert, Martin: *The Holocaust: The Jewish Tragedy* (Collins, 1986)

Gilbert, Martin: *Final Journey* (Allen & Unwin, 1979)

Gill, Anton: *The Journey Back from Hell: Conversations and Concentration Camp Survivors* (Grafton Books, 1988)

Keneally, Thomas: *Schindler's Ark* (Hodder and Stoughton, 1982)

Levi, Primo: *The Drowned and the Saved* (Abacus, 1988)

Lewis, Helen: *A Time to Speak* (Blackstaff Press, 1992)

Marks, Jane: *The Hidden Children* (Piatkus, 1994)

Shirer, William L.: *The Rise and Fall of the Third Reich* (Secker & Warburg, 1960)

Uris, Leon: *Exodus* (Alan Wingate, 1959)